5 THINGS SUCCESSFUL PEOPLE DO BEFORE 8 A.M.

TERRI SAVELLE FOY

978-1-942126-16-4

Terri Savelle Foy Ministries
Post Office Box 1959
Rockwall, TX 75087
www.terri.com

Printed in the United States of America

CONTENTS

INTRODUCTION

**"If we did all the things we are capable
of doing, we would literally
astound ourselves."
- Thomas Edison**

It was moving day November 22, 2014, when a 45-year-old woman
in a jogging suit and ponytail was carrying boxes into her new 6,000
square foot, European-style home. Located on a prestigious golf course
and landscaped pond in the wealthiest county in the state of Texas,
this new homeowner had authored five books, co-hosted a worldwide
television show, and spoke to hundreds of thousands of people each year
through her live appearances and popular YouTube channel.

She and her team had recently relocated their headquarters to this
new city, showcasing vision on every wall of the Parisian-decorated
offices. Her daughter had started her senior year of high school and was
pursuing a modeling career. Meanwhile, she and her entrepreneurial
husband recently celebrated 23 years of marriage. She had no debt. Her
cars were paid off. Her investment portfolio was growing, and she had
developed multiple streams of revenue. Her body wasn't perfect, but she
was physically active and fit with plenty of energy for the dreams ahead
of her.

Not to mention, her itinerary was full of upcoming speaking
engagements, another book was in the works and media buyers were
discussing the launch of her new television show.

As she carried another box of shoes into her new dream closet (the size of her master bedroom from years ago), a young woman hired by the professional cleaning company politely asked a life-changing question that became the focus of this entire book: "Ma'am, I want to know," she asked. "How do you get a life like this?"

Without hesitation, the successful, goal-oriented woman responded, "Your routine."

"Ma'am?" the young lady asked in a confused tone.

"If you'll change your routine, you can change your whole life," said the blessed homeowner.

Rewind to the fall of 2002, when that same woman at only 33 years of age would be totally unrecognizable compared to who she is today. On a rainy, September morning, she pulled into the driveway of her modest home in Crowley, Texas, walked in the back door of her clothing-piled laundry room, laid her keys on the cluttered kitchen counter, and looked around the empty house with overwhelm and dread.

What do I do now?

Where do I go from here?

Is this all there is to life?

Those were the thoughts racing through her mind as she stared into the stillness of nothing. Not a sound. Not an agenda. Not a calendar. Not even a to-do list. Other than raising her precious five-year-old daughter, she had nothing to look forward to, to reach for or to focus on. Each day was a repeat of the day before.

Recently separated from her husband, her world was falling apart. Life as she had known it for 11 years was coming to an end. Her daughter had started kindergarten and wasn't running around the house or going to the office by her side each day. Her job had changed when her boss asked her to temporarily work from home due to the emotional stress of her marriage. And her husband was living with his mom until the decision for divorce was made final. Nothing was normal.

She had credit card debt accumulated from years of overspending.

Car payments for both she and her husband, an empty savings account from spending everything they earned, nonexistent investment funds, and basically, nothing to show for her employment of more than a decade. She lived on fast food, never consumed water, and exercised only for special upcoming occasions such as spring break, summer vacation, or a big event.

Truthfully, it wasn't the sudden change of seasons in her life (her only child starting school or her husband kicked to the curb) that led to this solemn moment. It was an accumulation of subconscious habits and unsuccessful patterns over time that resulted in this boring, average, uninteresting, and dread-filled life.

For years, her days consisted of waking up at the last minute to go to work, jamming out to her favorite beats all the way to the office, grabbing her daily burrito at lunch (with a Texas-size sweet tea), and filling her evenings with hours of watching contestants phone-a-friend to become the next millionaire and women fighting over a rose ceremony. Only to do it again the next day.

What felt like sudden change in her life was really the result of more than a decade of poor habits. She looked around her house with disgust. She was miserable. She was visionless. And she felt as if she were hiding away from the world. *Does anybody know how depressed I am? Does anybody even care? How did my life end up like this?*

During this emotional season of self-pity and sadness, she didn't have a life coach come to her house and lay out a growth track for success. Nor did she have a minister lead her to the perfect scriptures for overcoming sorrow and misery. She didn't even have a book handy to guide her out of this pit. Since graduating from college, she'd never picked up another book, but now she was desperate. She was crying out for a solution, a vision, something to get up for each morning other than fix her daughter's pigtails and load the dishwasher.

Her solution was revealed in the most unspectacular fashion.

She grabbed a notebook and began to write down five things that popped into her mind. They were new habits she wanted to practice every day for the next 21 days.

At the end of the 21-day goal, something truly remarkable changed. Her.

Her mindset was improving. Her body was slimming. Her attitude was shifting. And her vision was emerging.

How could a notebook, a calendar, and a three-week goal transform a person so radically? It was during that first week or two that she heard the statement from leadership expert, John Maxwell, that explains the premise of this entire book: "The secret of your success is hidden in your daily routine."[1]

I like to say it this way, "The secret of your future is hidden in your daily *routine*."

Maxwell continued, "If I could come to your house and spend just one day with you, I would be able to tell whether or not you will be successful. You could pick the day. If I got up with you in the morning and went through the day with you, watching you for 24 hours, I could tell in what direction your life is headed."

Then, he explained why he would make such a bold claim. "You will never change your life until you change something you do *daily*. You see, success, doesn't suddenly occur one day in someone's life. For that matter, neither does failure. Each is a process. Every day of your life is merely preparation for the next. What you become is the result of what you do today."

That philosophy changed the trajectory of her life.

And the same can happen for you.

You may have guessed that this strawberry-blonde, ponytailed woman standing in a dream home, in a wealthy city, giving success advice is me. And so was the depressed, lonely, hopeless woman standing in an empty kitchen completely unaware that she was the reason she'd ended up in such extreme circumstances years earlier.

Please understand that this book is not to brag on my accomplishments or to take credit for the favor of God on my life. I don't want to imply that I've got it all together and my life is a piece of cake (although I do eat plenty of cake)! The truth is that I've had my share of hellacious struggles, disappointments, and heartbreak; however, my story is one of hope and inspiration of what is possible with a simple change in your daily routine.

You change yourself by changing something you do *each day*.

> ## "I've never met a person that was successful who didn't have a great amount of self-discipline."
> ### - John Maxwell

If you're in a rut, like I was, repeating the same story year after year, this book will lead you out.

If you've got big dreams for your life but don't know where to start on the journey of pursuing them, this book will become a manual for where to go next.

If you've tried to adapt good habits in the past only to fall back time and time again, the information inside this book will help you break those patterns.

If you feel somewhat disgusted with an aspect of your life, you're in the best place for change. Frustration is a sign of vision. Disgust can lead to a life change. Although we normally don't equate the word *disgust* with positive action, being repelled by your current circumstances can serve as vision and momentum to get out of them!

For example, seeing a photo of yourself overweight can disgust you so much that you declare, "I've had it! I'm making a change!" Having your debit card declined for insufficient funds can be enough disgust that you boldly claim, "That's it! I'm turning my life around!" Your electricity being shut off because you paid your bills late again can be the disgust that causes you to say, "I'm not living like this another day. I'm changing my habits."

This book is about taking 100% responsibility for where you are and where you're headed from this day forward. You will develop the number one skill needed to achieve a life of success: self-discipline.

In fact, Kurt Kopmeyer, who was a legend in the field of success and achievement, wrote about 1,000 success principles that he had observed from more than 50 years of research and study. Over lunch one day, success coach Brian Tracy asked him the question that everybody wants to know, "Of all the success principles that you have discovered, which do you think is the most important?"

Tracy said, "He smiled at me, with a twinkle in his eye, as if he had been asked this question many times, and replied without hesitating, 'There are 999 other success principles that I have found in my reading and experience, but without self-discipline, none of them work.'"[2]

"Do what you should do, when you should do it, whether you feel like it or not."
- Thomas Huxley

Self-discipline is the key to personal fulfillment. It is the key that opens doors for you that you never dreamed possible. With self-discipline, the ordinary person can become extraordinary, and the average person can rise further than talents and intelligence can take him. At the same time, without self-discipline, a talented, educated, attractive person will seldom rise above mediocrity.

Early in her career, author and minister Joyce Meyer asked a man who had been in ministry for over 40 years what advice he would give her to help stay focused and not allow challenges to convince her to quit along the way. His wise words of more than four decades of success were: "Whatever you did to get to where you're at, don't stop doing it."

Since 2002, I haven't stopped my five daily disciplines that have produced outstanding results in my life. The best part is they only take up about 20% of my entire day! I'm finished before breakfast.

My purpose and my prayer is that this book will help you:
- Seize the value of each day by taking control of your mornings.
- Establish a set of *realistic* habits that will revolutionize your life.
- Understand self-discipline and its importance in your life.
- Become aware of (and stop) your bad habits and their consequences.
- Discover your purpose and your life assignment so that you stay driven.

Bottom line: When you take control of your habits, you'll take control of your life.

MY DAILY ROUTINE

This is what I stick to on a daily basis when I'm home. Yes, things may vary 5-15 minutes from time-to-time, but I'm pretty rigid about keeping this schedule. When I travel for conferences and events, I am not usually in bed as early as I am when I'm home, so my wake time isn't always 4:45 a.m.

However, whatever time I need to be somewhere, I typically allow three hours to invest in myself before I invest in others. If I need to be somewhere at 10:00 a.m., I set the alarm to 6:45/7:00 a.m.

I am very protective of this schedule. I guard my time strictly. God has blessed me so much, and drastically changed me and everything around me. I view this routine as precious and priceless. It's something I'm honored to do rather than I'm forced to do. Getting up each day to invest in yourself is an opportunity, not an obligation. This perspective changes everything.

4:30 a.m.: First alarm sounds.

4:45 a.m.: Second alarm sounds. I get up. Brush teeth. Push play and listen to motivational messages while I put on my workout clothes, a little makeup (definitely mascara), and fix a ponytail.

5:10 a.m.: I'm in the kitchen taking vitamins, eating something light, drinking water, and ready to go work out.

5:15 a.m.: Leave for the gym. During my 10-minute commute, I spend time praying, worshiping God and making positive declarations.

5:25 a.m.: Work out. I'll do 30 minutes of weight-training and 30 minutes of cardio while listening to motivational messages on my phone.

6:40 a.m.: Pray and meditate. After returning home I go in my private study for quiet time with the Lord. What I do during this time is totally open to the Lord. Sometimes I read the Bible, journal my gratitude, worship Him, journal what I hear in my spirit, pray over my dreams and goals and/or make positive declarations. Or sometimes I just sit quietly and listen for however long I feel is necessary. Most days it's 20 minutes, but some days it could be hours. I try to be sensitive to the Lord and what I feel He's desiring of me.

7:00 a.m.: Read.

7:20 a.m.: Get dressed and ready to go.

8:00 a.m.: I'm out the door!

Throughout this book I've included morning routines and daily habits of some of my friends. They are all successful in their various roles and pursuits, and they all have a "Daily 5". I want you to see that successful people are intentional, but their routines are different based on their priorities.

1

STOP KILLING TIME

"Each day teaches us the value of time. Be grateful for the daily opportunities." - Malika E. Nura

If you had the choice today of eating a bucket of freshly-popped, buttery, lightly-salted popcorn or being given a set of car keys to drive the car of your dreams, (do I even need to ask) which would you take? Let's also assume that you are famished. You are wilting of hunger under the sweltering temperatures of hot South Africa and at the sight of this mouth-watering popcorn, you are drooling with desire. Would you still resist the sheer, old-fashioned taste of this now caramel-drizzled popcorn for a set of dangling metal? The sad truth is that more people choose the popcorn over the car keys every single day. I'll explain.

A friend of mine went on an adventurous trip to South Africa. While most tourists choose to experience the typical safari, getting a view of the Big Five in this majestic land (the lion, leopard, rhinoceros, elephant and buffalo), my friend chose to see the monkeys. These cute, little monkeys were in a sanctuary, free to roam about the tree-covered hills and acreage spreading as far as the eye could see. *But* these weren't your regular monkeys. These small primates were going through rehab.

Yes, they were adorable...but also little criminals.

These monkeys were rescued from thieves. Crooks would train these monkeys to appear innocent and inviting, but while they're captivating you and sucking their thumb, they were craftily sliding your ring off your finger, slipping a hand in your back pocket to take your phone, your wallet or your car keys. They were felons! These were outlaw monkeys. True story.

So, before my friends toured the sanctuary, the guide gave them strict warning, "Don't take anything valuable into the sanctuary. Do not take your phone, your car keys, your wallet, your jewelry, or your purse."

My friends asked, "Seriously?"

The guide warned, "Yes!" He said, "Last week, we had a guy who was given this warning, but he did not listen. He took his car keys with him, and sure enough, the monkey stole 'em right out of his pocket."

One of the alarmed tourists asked, "How did you get them back?"

The guide answered, "Popcorn!"

"Popcorn?"

"Yes, monkeys love popcorn! We toss the kernels of popcorn on the ground and without fail, the monkeys come and eat it all," said the guide. "But then, I leave one kernel in my hand and when they see everything else is devoured, they run up to a single piece in desperation. I hold up the last kernel and say, 'If you want the popcorn, you have to give me the keys.' Without fail, the monkey will drop the car keys, take the popcorn, and run off!"

There is an important truth in this monkey business. That monkey has in his possession something incredibly valuable. Those car keys have the potential to change his life. Pretend with me for a moment. With the car keys, that monkey could go anywhere he wants. He could drive to the popcorn store. He could sell the car and buy all the popcorn he wants. He has the ability to floor it, get out of that monkey prison, and be free! But he drops it all for one single kernel of popcorn that's gone in five seconds!

Popcorn vs. Car Keys

Did you know that most people your age, ("What age are you talking about?" you might ask. *Your age*. Whatever your age is, 22, 35, 47, 63, most people *your age*) will pick popcorn over car keys? They'll choose a short-term desire over a long-term destiny! They pick entertainment over wisdom. Instant gratification versus delayed reward. What is that? It's popcorn over car keys.

You can go to a bookstore and pick up a gossip magazine (popcorn) and miss out on a personal development book (car keys) that could catapult your life to a whole new level. You can sit down and watch TV (popcorn) instead of listening to one podcast (car keys) that could take your business to soaring new heights. You can scroll for two hours on Facebook (popcorn) while missing a webinar (car keys) that could give you an idea to triple your income.

That used to be me. I was a popcorn kind of girl. I was average. I drove an average car. Lived in an average house. Worked an average job for an average salary. The only area I was consistent in was consistently choosing popcorn over car keys (short-term desires over long-term destiny).

As I mentioned in the introduction, my days were comprised of pushing the snooze button until the last minute, pulling up to work barely on time, and ending the day consumed with watching other people live their dreams as I watched episode after episode on my couch (aka eating popcorn). For more than a decade!

When I first started my five daily habits, I heard this phrase in my prayer time and penned it in my journal, "Don't be average and your life won't be average." (Emphasis on the understood *you* in that command:

You don't be average and your life won't be average!) In other words, if everyone else is choosing popcorn, you choose the car keys!

I can humbly and gratefully say today, I no longer drive an average car. I don't live in an average house. I don't earn an average salary. I don't speak at average conferences, and I don't serve an average God. I learned how to choose car keys over popcorn, and I want to show you how you can too.

The Clock is Ticking

It all comes down to how you are spending every precious and valuable second of your day. First, identify where you are killing time and don't even realize it.

Let's imagine a bank credits your account each morning with $86,400. And each evening, it cancels out whatever amount you didn't spend during the day. You can't carry any leftover balance, but you get another deposit the next morning of $86,400. How would you handle this? You would utilize every cent every day, wouldn't you? You would be adamant about making sure you got all that you were entitled to and nothing was wasted.

Well, you do have a similar bank, and it's called a clock. Your time is the most valuable thing you have. Every single morning, it credits you with 86,400 seconds. Each night, whatever you didn't use effectively is gone forever. You can't get it back. It's your loss. But you get to start over with a fresh deposit the next morning.

What am I saying? The clock is ticking. When you view your time differently, you'll start making the most of it. Every second counts. Each of the 150 times you check your Instagram post counts. Each time you plop down in front the television for three hours counts. Every time you get into a debate on Facebook counts. Each morning you oversleep by thirty minutes counts. These are seconds, minutes, and hours that turn into days, weeks, months, and years of your life being wasted.

These are precious moments that you could be sightseeing the countries you've dreamed of visiting, writing your life story in a book to pass on to your great-grandchildren, brainstorming ideas that could move you into a whole new tax bracket, or walking in your neighborhood to improve your health.

We are killing time every day without even knowing it. On average, we waste 10 minutes a day simply looking for our car keys and/or cell phone in the morning. That's five hours a month! The average person oversleeps by 30 minutes every morning. That's 10 hours a month! We scroll social media sites an average of 50 minutes each day. That's 25 hours a month![3] And we're stuck in traffic up to 42 hours a year![4]

In each account of time wasted, the hours add up to days, and the days lead to years of our lives flying by with nothing to show for it.

Bottom line: you have a limited number of seconds to do something with your life. How you choose to spend them results in how you spend your life.

The average life expectancy in America is 78.6 years. You may be surprised by some of the funny but true ways we spend the years of our lives.

- 28.3 years sleeping
- 10.5 years working
- 9 years watching TV, playing video games, or on social media
- 6 years doing chores
- 4 years eating and drinking
- 3.5 years on education
- 2.5 years getting ready (grooming ourselves)
- 2.5 years shopping
- 1.5 years caring for children
- 1.3 years commuting[5]

After all that, you have only 9 years to live your dreams. Alarming, isn't it? Well, an alarm is meant to wake us up. I want you to wake up to the reality that you don't have time to waste. You don't have another hour to kill, another morning to snooze, or another year to squander. Your time is precious, and each day spent wasting your time is you wasting your life.

"Lost time is never found again."
- Benjamin Franklin

Life coach and counselor, Vicki Tillman says she has three types of clients:
1. Millennials – when they turn 30 and realize their young adulthood is gone, and they have nothing to show for it.
2. Generation X'ers – when they turn 45 and realize that many opportunities they'd hoped for are lost, so what is left?
3. Boomers – when they hit 60 or retirement and realize that their satisfaction with life is so much less than they had expected, what happens now?[6]

Tillman says, "These realities create moments of fear, despair or regret."

The 5 Common Regrets of the Dying

Bronnie Ware, a hospice nurse from Australia, had the honor of being a caregiver of elderly patients in the last three to twelve weeks of their lives. She noticed a common theme of great remorse among those nearing the end. Her role as a caregiver became more about listening to their dying epiphanies than anything. With more clarity than they had in their early years, they revealed their deepest sorrows as they neared the end of their lives.

There was no mention of wishing for working longer hours at the office or even making a million dollars. Quite the opposite. As much of her time was spent in silence sitting bedside with her aging patients, she began to journal their intimate discussions.

Here are the five most common regrets confessed to her.

1. "I wish I'd had the courage to live a life true to myself, not the life others expected of me."

Ware reports, "This was *the most common* regret of all."

In the words of the late Myles Munroe, "The richest place in the world isn't the diamond mines of South Africa or the oil fields of the Middle East. The wealthiest place in all the world is the graveyard." Buried in the graveyard are books never written, songs never sung, businesses never started. Don't go to the grave with your dreams still in you!

"When people realize that their life is almost over and look back clearly on it," said Ware, "it is easy to see how many dreams have gone unfulfilled. Most people had not honoured even a half of their dreams and had to die knowing that it was due to choices they had made, or not made. Health brings a freedom that few realize, until they no longer have it."

Live your dreams while you still can.

2. "I wish I didn't work so hard."

"This came from *every male patient* that I nursed," said Ware. Although some women did share this regret, because her patients were from an older generation, many female patients did not work outside the home. But the men felt they had missed out on their children's youth and the companionship of their partner.

3. "I wish I'd had the courage to express my feelings."

Many of Ware's elderly patients suppressed their feelings wanting to keep peace and not 'rock the boat'; however, not voicing their true emotions led to great resentment. "As a result," said Ware, "they settled for a mediocre existence and never became who they were truly capable of becoming." Consequently, Ware reported that many of them developed illnesses relating to the bitterness and resentment they carried.

4. "I wish I had stayed in touch with my friends."

Many of her dying patients regretted getting so caught up in their own lives that they let golden friendships slip away through the years. "Often they would not truly realize the full benefits of old friends until their dying weeks, and it was not always possible to track them down." Ware added, "Everyone misses their friends when they are dying."

5. "I wish that I had let myself be happier."

Ware was surprised by this commonality among her patients saying, "Many did not realize until the end that happiness is a choice. They had stayed stuck in old patterns and habits. The so-called comfort of familiarity overflowed into their emotions, as well as their physical lives. Fear of change had them pretending to others, and to themselves, that they were content. When deep within, they longed to laugh properly and have silliness in their life again." Ware concludes, "When you are on your deathbed, what others think of you is a long way from your mind. How wonderful to be able to let go and smile again, long before you are dying."[7]

**"Regret for wasted time is
more wasted time"
- Mason Cooley**

This book was not written to fill your mind with regrets; I wrote it to put a fire under you to start truly living the life you were designed to live and enjoy it to the fullest. I am convinced that it starts by a simple change every day.

Deep down you know your life is meant to be something more. That's evident by you picking up this book. In these pages, I am going to help you start with a single step in the right direction that will lead you up a staircase to new heights.

Expired or Expedited: It's Up to You

A couple weeks ago, I was packing for a quick getaway trip to Cozumel, Mexico with my husband, Rodney. He had been asking me for months to take some time off and go relax on the beach. I finally found a few days to play and started packing my swimsuits and flip-flops.

As I grabbed our passports, I opened them to be certain I had the right ones and to ensure they weren't expired (or Rodney would be poolside by himself). I happened to notice my daughter, Kassidi's passport was in fact, expiring the next day! I phoned her and told her she needed to renew her passport as soon as possible knowing she would be joining me for a ministry trip to London, Amsterdam, and France in three months. You can imagine her utter relief when I called her realizing she could have missed an amazing opportunity simply because of an expiration date.

Think about that. She had plans to go to Europe. She had the finances to go. She had the desire to go. She was expecting to go. But she could have missed out on a trip of a lifetime because the deadline came and went. If she had waited, she would have missed out and been too late.

I don't want you to come to the end of your life and realize it's too late. That your expiration date is here. That you didn't get to enjoy what God wanted you to enjoy because you weren't ready. That your dreams remained in a drawer overlooked month after month, year after year, until your time expired.

In Kassidi's case, we had to fill out a special form to get the passport *expedited*. That word means "to hasten, to move quicker and faster." She didn't waste any time. Once she realized what needed to be done, she acted promptly. Time was of the essence, and she couldn't afford to delay another day. Because of her split-second decision to get things in motion with the passport office, as I write this chapter right now, I am sitting at a table in a little apartment in London, England while Kassidi is out walking around Hyde Park. Look at the opportunities and life experiences she is having because she took action.

Passport to Life

The truth is we all have an expiration date. Your time here on earth is limited. It's precious. It's valuable. God doesn't want you wasting another second with meaningless habits that are derailing your dreams. What if God placed a big stamp on our "passport to life" showing us how much time we have left? I mean, it's sorta creepy, but it would certainly motivate us to live each day with purpose.

When you think about the average lifespan (of an American) being 78.6 years as we talked about earlier, that means that if you are 42 years old, you only have 36 more Christmases left with your family. If you are 57 years old, you only have 21 more summers to enjoy at the lake. If you're 63 years old, that's 15 more birthday cakes with your family. Fifteen! That's nothing! It makes you view life more seriously, doesn't it?

First Corinthians 2:9 says, "No eye has seen, no ear has heard and no mind has imagined what God has prepared for those who love him" (NLT).

God has *prepared* an extraordinary life for you like I prepared to take Kassidi to Europe with me. Don't wait for your expiration date and miss out. It's time to wake up and really start living life. Start by making the seconds, the minutes, and the hours count.

I wasted years of my life accomplishing very little and repeating the same scenario year after year. But I made a decision to take the first step in a positive direction. I listened to the first message. I read the first chapter. I attended the first conference. I walked the first mile. Little by little, my mindset improved, my relationships strengthened, my dreams enlarged, and my body reshaped.

Every good decision pays off. I'm not wasting another second of my life living in that rut again, and I pray this book is your first step into your promising future.

How to Tell If You Are Wasting Your Life

Can you really be wasting your life if you are always going and doing? Busy doesn't equal productive. Let me remove any question you may have as to whether or not you need to make some big changes. Here are eight ways to tell if you are wasting your life.

MY DAILY ROUTINE

Chris Goodman
President/CEO of OpenRoad Lending
Daily 5:

1. Wake up and read a short devotional.

2. Go workout.

3. Have a protein shake and snack on the way to the office.

4. Review the day's tasks and ask the Lord to guide each step.

5. Share and pour into others as the "real" day starts.

1. You're comfortable.

How long has it been since you challenged yourself to learn something, to read, to grow, or to try something new? Being content is fine, but don't confuse contentedness with settling for less because you're too afraid or too lazy to go after what you really want.

Steve Jobs said that every single day he would look himself in the mirror and ask this question, "If today was the last day of my life, would I be happy with what I'm about to do?"[8] If his answer was *no* for too many days in a row, he knew he needed to make a change. This kind of inquiry causes you to view your daily decisions and actions in a new light. When your answer is *no* consistently, it becomes harder to ignore. You realize change is a must.

I was comfortable for 11 years. I drove the same route to work. I worked in the same office space at the same desk doing the same tasks for a decade. There's nothing wrong with that, especially if you love what you're doing, but I wasn't stretching myself out of my comfort zone. I wasn't committed to any kind of plan for personal growth. Because I was stagnant, everything in my life was stagnant. My savings account didn't increase. My relationships didn't grow. My life experiences didn't improve. When you stop growing, everything around you stops growing too.

In Genesis, we see the story of Abraham and his father, Terah, who set out for Canaan Land. *Canaan* means "the land of abundance or the land of more than enough." Many people are familiar with Abraham, but most can't recall the name of his dad. Why is that? The Bible reports that they both *set out* for Canaan Land. In other words, they both had every intention of making Canaan their destination.

What was the difference between Abraham and Terah? Genesis 11:31 says, Terah "stopped at Haran and settled there" (NLT). Think about the two words chosen to describe Terah: *stopped and settled*. He never made it to the land of abundance, fulfilled dreams, and more than enough, because he stopped and settled.

Don't let that be your story. You had every intention of writing that book, but you stopped along the way and settled. You had big goals to travel the world, but you stopped along the way and settled. You had great aspirations of having your own business, but you stopped along the way and settled.

Never stop and settle when God has so much more for your life!

Comfort and convenience run the lives of unsuccessful people. When I'm faced with making big decisions, I ask myself, "Terri, does this make you uncomfortable?" If the answer is yes, then I commit to doing it. The best thing you can do for yourself is purposefully put yourself in situations that force you to grow! Being uncomfortable is a good sign that you're headed down the road to success.

2. You've settled at a miserable job.

A typical eight-hour job makes up 1/3 of your daily life. We saw earlier in the account of a 78.6-year lifespan that working takes up 10.5 years of your entire existence. Why would you invest so much of your precious time doing something you hate?

In his article titled, "Stop Wasting Your Life," Paul Cummings recalls a coaching session he had with a young executive who was miserable in her career.

"What do you enjoy most about your work?" Cummings asked.

"Every day when I get to leave," said the young executive.

"Then, why have you stayed for five years if you are unhappy?" asked Cummings.

"I thought maybe I could learn to like what I do if I gave it enough time," she replied.

When he asked what first attracted her to this line of work, the woman answered, "It's what I studied in college, and I didn't want to waste my degree."

His response was bold and candid, "You are not wasting your degree or the money and time you invested in your education. You are wasting your time, your energy, your talent, and as a result, you are depriving yourself of your most important goals and dreams. You need to make a better decision: *Stop wasting your life*!"[9]

Life is not a dress rehearsal. We aren't afforded a do-over just in case this life doesn't pan out the way we dreamed it would. We get one shot to go full-speed ahead at living the life God intended us to live and more importantly, fulfilling the assignment He's given us to fulfill.

Unfortunately, this scenario described by Paul Cummings and the unhappy executive is happening to 80% of Americans who claim to be miserable in their careers.[10] Yet no matter how much they despise the work they chose, they still get up one dreadful day after another and watch the clock tick.

Think about that phrase, "watch the clock tick." They are literally watching their expiration date (on their passport to life) draw nearer and nearer with each miserable second they have remaining. That is no way to live your valuable life. Stop killing time doing work that doesn't engage your brilliance, ignite your passion, and motivate you to jump out of bed in the morning.

3. Your TV is your BFF.

The average American watches over five hours of TV a day![11] That's over 35 hours a week in front of a TV set or as I like to say, watching other people live their dreams.

Is your TV time aiding you to a better life? Is it getting you closer to your goals?

The results are shocking when you transfer one hour of TV time to doing something productive. You will be amazed at what you can accomplish in 60 minutes: clean an entire room, read a couple chapters, walk off a few hundred calories, become more fluent in a new language, learn a new lesson, brainstorm an idea that could change your life.

You may think you're spending a couple hours each night as you unwind, but I encourage you to track it this week. I think you will be as surprised as I was years ago to discover exactly how much time you spend watching television.

Time wasters are subtle. You don't realize how much is wasted and dwindled away a little at a time. Remember, your time is your life. If you waste your time, you waste your life.

4. You make excuses.

> **"He that is good for making excuses is seldom good for anything else."**
> **- Benjamin Franklin**

Excuses are the subtle reasons we justify ourselves when we don't want to admit that we are where we are because of our choices. The truth is we can always find ground not to pursue our goals. After all, our reasons are *reasonable*. George Washington Carver said, "Ninety-nine percent of the failures come from people who have the habit of making excuses."

They say that if you really want something, you will find a way. If you don't, you'll find an excuse why you can't succeed. "Excuses are mainly a means of placing the blame of an internal problem on an external condition,"[12] says life coach Adam Sicinski.

In other words, every excuse you can make has a counteraction you can take. Whether it's the excuse of:

I don't have the education. Learn more.
Nobody believes in me. Believe in yourself.
It's never been done before. Be the first.
I'm too busy. Schedule time.

It's too hard. Anything worth having doesn't come easy.

I've made too many mistakes. Forgive yourself and move on.

It's too late. Focus on the time you have left and use it wisely.

This isn't the right time. And it never will be if you keep making excuses.

They are so easy to make. Excuses are a sign that you want to do better, but you also don't want to be uncomfortable. You have to ask yourself, "How badly do I want _____?" When you truly desire a goal or a dream, you will eliminate any excuse and rise to the occasion to achieve it. Taking responsibility for where you are in life at this moment is your foundation for success. It means you accept responsibility for the things you do and the things you fail to do. Living an excuse-free life starts you on the pathway to success.

Nearly everything worthwhile in life comes with great challenges. Never justify why you can't succeed by making excuses. Embrace the journey, challenge yourself, learn new things, be vulnerable, stick your neck out, stop playing it safe, and prove to yourself that you have what it takes to succeed in life.

5. You relive the good ol' days.

Do you feel like your best days are behind you? If you are still talking about what you did yesterday, you haven't done much today. When you dwell on the past, you remain in the past. This mindset can make you lose sight of where God wants to take you. It can mess up your present, cause you to pass up incredible opportunities, and steal your ability to enjoy the life God has arranged for you to live.

Author Ann Landers said, "Some people believe holding on and hanging in there are signs of great strength. However, there are times when it takes much more strength to know when to let go and then do it." Her words provide wisdom to let go of the past and start living in the present. Everything God has for you is ahead of you not behind you. Yes, be grateful for whatever good memories you made and successes you acquired, but your greatest assignment is before you.

There's a verse in the gospel of Luke that is simply three words: "Remember Lot's wife" (Luke 17:32, NIV). If you are familiar with the original story in Genesis, then you know that God was getting ready to destroy the city of Sodom and Gomorrah because of the sin that was running rampant. It broke God's heart to see all these people He created to love Him were doing nothing but looking for new ways to sin and rebel against Him.

God promised to save Lot and his family from the city's destruction but gave them one command: Don't look back!

Lot's wife did the exact thing God said not to do! She looked back. When she did, she was turned into a pillar of salt. Turning back gave the impression that she cared more about her past than she did her future. In other words, she lost her future by looking back!

"Escape for your life! Do not look behind you!"
- Genesis 19:17

You, too, can lose your future by looking back! When your memories are bigger than your dreams, it kills your today. This is a serious issue. Are you spending more time rehearsing the past than planning for the future? I don't know about you, but I don't want to come to the end of my life and have nothing but regret. I don't want people saying, "She had a lot of potential, but she lived in the past." I want to do all that God wants me to do and have all that He wants me to have, and I believe you do too or you wouldn't pick up a book about success.

Frank Lloyd Wright, the architect famous for designing the Guggenheim Museum and many other historical masterpieces, was asked at 80+ years old which was his favorite of all his creations. He replied, "My next one!" He understood the concept of always having a vision, a dream, a goal before you no matter how good the good ol' days were.

Rather than surround yourself only with memories of the past—the graduation photos, the wedding pictures, and the albums full of family vacations—start surrounding yourself with where you're headed. Get a vision board and pin photos of exciting places you want to visit, goals you want to achieve, and new adventures you plan to take. Make your dreams bigger than your memories.

6. You've stopped dreaming.

This point ties in with my last one. The bottom line is, that a person with no vision will always return to their past. You must have a dream of where you want to go or you'll wind up right back where you are today. While it's always great to live in the now and be present in the moment, you also need to look ahead to see where you want to go in the future.

Imagine it's pouring down rain outside, and you jump in your car to drive home. Your engine works properly, the heater is working fine, the lights turn on, the music is pumping, but the windshield wipers seem to be broken. Guess what? You're not going anywhere. If you can't see out the front windshield in a thunderstorm, you are stuck in place. As long as your vision is impaired, you will stay where you are. You need your own inner GPS to know where you are going and to guide you to your destination.

Having no dream for your life is a time waster. God tells us, "Where there is no vision, the people perish" (Proverbs 29:18, KJV). *Perish* means die. If you're going around day to day with no dream on the inside of you, you're like a dead man walking.

You may have stopped dreaming because you think you don't have a passion, but that's never the case. There must be something that you enjoy doing. It's time to rediscover what excites you, and then do more of it. If you have a goal of doing something "someday," that day is today. The more you put it off, the more you'll never check it off. (I will share more on this topic in Chapter 6.)

What have you always dreamed of doing?
- Learn how to cook
- Read 100 books
- Travel to 10 countries
- Climb 5 mountains
- Enjoy weekend getaways with your best friends
- Run in your local marathon
- Make a scrapbook of your life
- Learn a foreign language
- Start investing 10% of your income
- Read the entire Bible
- Give a speech
- Volunteer at a local shelter or safe house
- Go on a mission trip to an underprivileged country

There is so much for you to look forward to. Don't ever stop dreaming. Don't ever stop pursuing your vision.

7. You've stopped learning.

When you stop growing, you start dying. In these pages, you will discover that you have plenty of opportunities every day to learn something new and to grow yourself. When you do, everything around you will grow with you. Your income, your relationships, your opportunities, your connections, your career, etc.

The truth is that when you stop feeding your mind, as I did for 11 years after college, you become stagnant. Jim Rohn, the great motivator and thought leader, was blaming everyone for where he was in life: stuck, broke, full of excuses, nothing in the bank, and pennies in his pocket. Until his wealthy mentor, Earl Shoaf, told him, "If you want the future to change, you've got to change."[13] And that change can begin by picking up one book, listening to one podcast, or attending one conference.

View your growth as a *way* of life, not a *period* of life. The dawn of every day brings us an opportunity to make improvements to our lives. An interesting thing happens when you start the journey of personal growth: The more you learn, the hungrier you are to learn more. You can't get enough. You begin to crave knowledge and wisdom as much as you used to crave sitting on a couch vegging out to reality shows. Why? You start experiencing the rewards of what you're learning.

Jim Rohn said, "You cannot change your destination overnight, but you can change your direction overnight. If you want to reach your goals and fulfill your potential, become intentional about your personal growth. It *will* change your life."[14]

8. You don't believe in yourself.

What you believe about yourself on the inside is what you will manifest on the outside. As Henry Ford said, "Whether you think you can, or think you can't…either way, you're right." If you tell yourself that you're not good enough to have your own business, then you're right. If you tell yourself you're too old to start achieving your goals, then you're right. If you tell yourself that you're not qualified to get that promotion, then you won't. Whatever you tell yourself becomes your reality.

Closely monitor what you say to yourself, because when you fill your mind with positive thoughts, your life will line up with it.

> **"When you write the story of your life—don't let anyone else hold the pen."**
> **- Unknown**

The truth is you didn't get to choose which country you were born in, which city you grew up in, the parents you were born to, or the environment you were raised in. You didn't even get to choose the name you would be called for a lifetime. Although you didn't get to choose the beginning of your story, you have everything to do with how your story ends!

One day, you're going to wake up on your 78th birthday, and as you look back on the life you've lived, are you going to smile at what you see? Will you be proud of the legacy you created? Will you wish you hadn't *stopped and settled* somewhere along the way? If a caregiver were sitting by your side with a journal and pen listening to your final thoughts, what would fill up the pages of her diary? Whatever remorse there would be, let it become your driving inspiration to change now.

Are you going to pursue your dreams or complain about what could have been? Settle or strive? Rest or reach? The choice is entirely up to you.

Here's the good part: all you need to start a drastic change in the right direction is (1) the will and (2) a watch. Time is ticking so let's start the countdown to your new routine.

> **"Don't just aspire to make a living; aspire to make a difference."**
> **- Denzel Washington**[15]

21

MY DAILY ROUTINE

Sandra Goodman

Wife, mom, Mary-Kay consultant

Daily 5:

1. Coffee first.

2. Read the verse for the day.

3. Read the news headlines.

4. Pray for our President and nation.

5. Personal devotion and prayer time.

2

THE 5 MORNING HABITS FOR A SUCCESSFUL LIFE

**"Motivation is what gets you started.
Habit is what keeps you going."
- Jim Rohn**

What do Oprah Winfrey, Lady Gaga, Mick Jagger, and Terri Savelle Foy have in common? Other than loving heavy eyeliner, we all have *morning* rituals and routines that have led us to our dreams. Before most people have even taken the Pop-Tart out of the toaster, high-achievers have typically read two chapters, jogged two miles, and heard two mentors give exceptional advice.

I didn't realize (until 2002) that each morning I lost the battle of the bed took me further from success. Each morning that I slept an extra 30 minutes was compounding to an extra 10 hours each month that could change my life or keep me stuck.

The most successful people in the world have something in common: They practice mind over mattress. They conquer the covers! From political leaders and ministers, to famous athletes, CEOs, and celebrities, they cherish the morning hours to get up and invest in themselves while the rest of the world chooses to snooze.

Arnold Schwarzenegger said, "People say, 'I need 8-10 hours of sleep.' No. Sleep a little faster! Make the most of the hours you have each day!"

I like to think of this change in mindset like a car stuck in the mud. You need just enough traction to move an inch; then you can gain momentum to move out and move on. That's what happens when you start waking up a little earlier each day. It's the shove you need to gain that traction to catapult you miles ahead of where you need to be.

Benjamin Franklin said, "Early to bed and early to rise makes a man healthy, wealthy, and wise." More than 200 years later, early risers are still among the most productive, wealthy, and successful people. Waking up early enables you to take control of your day first thing in the morning rather than the day controlling you.

Waking up one hour earlier each day would give you an extra 15 days each year. What could you accomplish with an extra two weeks added to your life every year? Take an inventory of your current routine. You already have one, but the question is, does it support your goals? Is it helping you get closer to where you want to be? Are you waking up with determination and even better, going to sleep with satisfaction that you seized the last 24 hours? Or are you in that place I was in for 11 years of waking up frantic, rushing, trying to dash out the door hoping you haven't forgotten anything and going to sleep feeling dissatisfied with all the to-do's left undone on the list?

The morning is a particularly critical time, whether you're a morning person or not. How you start the day can affect your mood and productivity throughout the day. Your morning sets the tone for the rest of the day and positions you to succeed before interruptions begin.

Check out the morning rituals of the following successful people:

- Bill Gates, founder of Microsoft, starts each day out with one hour on the treadmill while watching educational teaching.

- Howard Schultz, former CEO of Starbucks, wakes up at 4:30 a.m., walks his dogs, and works out.
- Richard Branson, founder of Virgin enterprise, leaves his curtains open, so when the sun comes up at 5:45 a.m., he rises with it. His routine consists of playing tennis with someone younger and more fit than him or swimming around his island before eating a healthy breakfast.
- Jack Dorsey, founder of Twitter, wakes up at 5:30 a.m., meditates, and jogs for six miles.
- Mick Jagger, lead singer of the Rolling Stones, credits his morning ritual of working out six days a week to helping him reduce stress and keep up his stamina.
- Lady Gaga begins each morning with yoga as well as five minutes of self-directed love.
- Stephen King begins each day with a glass of water or tea, takes his vitamins, listens to music, and sits in the same seat to help him clear his mind and be more focused.

As you can see from this list of familiar names, it doesn't matter what profession a person pursues, a morning routine is key to success. While the average person rolls over, the high performer rolls out and gets a jump start on the day. Could you imagine if you woke up on purpose with purpose every morning?

Fitness guru, Jack LaLanne, hosted the longest running, on air fitness program, *The Jack LaLanne Show*, for 34 years. It's no surprise that he had a ritual which led him to prominent success. At the age of 94, he was still working out two hours a day with 90 minutes of weightlifting and 30 minutes of cardio. He was fond of saying, "I cannot afford to die. It will ruin my image." Your repetition is your reputation.

Why is the morning the greatest time to establish a success routine?

In the morning hours, you have the most control over your day. You can be most productive first thing in the morning because people and priorities haven't invaded your attention. Willpower is at its highest in the morning. The longer the day goes on, the more fatigued we become.

Your morning affects your outlook on the rest of the day. Start the day feeling productive and accomplished. Invest in YOU before you invest in everything and everyone else.

Join the 5 a.m. Club

Successful people are proactive about their day—not reactive. They take care of themselves first before they attend to those around them.

On every airplane flight I've ever been on, before the pilot takes off, the flight attendant explains the "in case of emergency" procedures. Notice, they always caution you to put your oxygen mask on first before you attend to anyone else, even small children. Once your mask is in place, you are able to assist other passengers. It's the same with your daily agenda. Once you've invested in yourself first thing in the morning, you are well-prepared to invest in those around you.

Bestselling author Jon Acuff tells how the only way he could learn to be consistent in his personal growth (in addition to working a full-time job and raising a family with his wife) was to start "being selfish at 5:00 a.m." He began the discipline of getting up at the crack of dawn to read, to listen to messages, to journal, to write and to pray. He reported that since he began this early morning ritual, "Not one time has my wife complained that I wasn't spending time with her at 5 a.m. Not one time has my daughter asked me to ride bikes with her at 5 a.m. nor has my other daughter asked me to jump rope." He says, "That's *your* time to focus on you, your personal development. Own your mornings."

If the idea of setting your alarm 30 minutes earlier for you sounds horrible, then you may not be ready to get out of a rut, to rise above average, and to live your dreams. Jon Acuff challenges, "If your dream isn't worth 30 minutes, you've either got the wrong dream or you're just pretending you have one."

That's the realization I had to come to if I was ever going to change my life. In fact, I heard someone define the word *poor* as "Passing Over Opportunities Repeatedly." You might say, "But, Terri, that's just it. I haven't had any opportunities." My argument is this: Yes, you have. Every morning at 5:00 a.m. (or 6:00 or 7:00), you have another opportunity to get up and invest in your future. What you commit to each hour is building your future.

Legendary motivator Zig Ziglar encouraged goal-oriented people to replace the term "alarm clock" (which is negative) with the word "opportunity clock" (which is positive). Immediately, when the "opportunity clock" goes off, your mind is headed in a positive direction about what the day will bring!

Notice the wake-up calls for these high-achievers:
- Xerox CEO gets up at 5:15 a.m.
- Chrysler CEO gets up at 3:30 a.m.
- General Motors' CEO rarely sleeps past 4:30 or 5:00 a.m.
- Apple CEO gets up at 4:30 a.m.
- AOL CEO gets up at 5:00 or 5:15 a.m.
- Disney CEO gets up 4:30 a.m.
- PepsiCo CEO gets up at 4:00 a.m.
- Brooklyn Nets CEO gets up at 3:30 a.m.
- Oxygen Channel CEO gets up at 6:00 a.m.

You don't have to get up before sunrise, but those who wake up early on a consistent basis are more productive than others who sleep late. Start this new routine by setting your alarm 20–30 minutes earlier than normal.

Author Tom Corley conducted an in-depth, five-year study documenting the daily activities of 233 wealthy people and 128 people living in poverty. He discovered more than 50% of wealthy people wake up three or more hours before they go to work.[16] Why? To invest in themselves. Conversely, only 3% of the poor people surveyed arose early to contribute to their goals.

You may have seen me post on Instagram: "*Obsessed* is a word the lazy use to describe the disciplined." Be prepared for people to call you "addicted, workaholic, insane, obsessed, etc.," but just smile and go back to setting your morning alarm because pretty soon they'll call you "boss, CEO, President, Mayor, Principal, successful!"

First Decision of the Day

Morning rituals can change your life and lead you to success. Now that we understand successful people wake up earlier than most, what are they doing after they beat the sun up? Are there certain habits that successful people have in common? If you applied these habits, could your life drastically change?

Before I answer that question, let me ask you this, how can you expect to achieve your goals when the first decision you make each morning is to procrastinate by hitting the snooze button?

When most people hear success stories, they only see how the person looks after they're successful. It's easy to get inspired and motivated by their achievements, but if you really want to learn from someone's success, then you need to learn how they got there. You need to know what they're doing in private that promoted them in public.

A Journey of Continuing

My father, Jerry Savelle, felt called into the ministry back in 1969. He knew he needed to prepare as much as possible to deliver sermons that could impact lives. His preparation included learning God's Word, reading the Bible, and studying it intensely.

One day, he came across a familiar scripture in John 8:31–32 that reads, "If you continue in my word, then are you my disciples (disciplined ones) indeed, you shall know the truth and the truth shall make you free" (KJV). Although he had read that verse many times before, this time, the word *continue* stood out as the biggest word on the page. He thought, "That's my problem! I quit everything. I quit college. I quit working at the Chevrolet dealership. I quit working at the Ford dealership. I quit the Mercury dealership. When things don't go my way, I quit. I've never *continued* anything."

In that moment, my dad began the journey of *continuing* by disciplining himself. He was so undisciplined about getting up early, at the time, but he knew he had to start investing in himself if he was ever going to pursue his big dream! So, he set the alarm for 6:00 a.m. the next morning. The alarm sounded, he got up immediately full of determination, walked into his guest bedroom, laid across the bed with his Bible open, and began reading. An hour later, he woke up!

This routine repeated itself day after day until he got so frustrated, he realized the bed was too tempting; he needed to sit up in a chair. Unfortunately, the chair was equally as cozy, and it rocked him right to sleep. Desperate for change in his life and his habits, he was so determined to continue that he walked in his bathroom, stood on the edge of the bathtub (literally, balancing himself), holding his Bible in his hands saying, "Jerry Savelle, you better not fall asleep or you're gonna bust your head! You better continue!"

That was the beginning of a lifetime of discipline.

This comical, but life-changing story of desperation worked! My dad is one of the most disciplined persons I know! His resolute decision back in 1969 to change his habits has resulted in establishing offices all over the world, airing a television broadcast in over 200 nations, authoring over 70 books, ministering in thousands of churches in nations across the globe…because he continued!

What you do every day is far more important than what you do every decade.

Creatures of Habit

Successful people are simply those with successful habits. To change your life, change your habits.

Habits are some of the most powerful forces that easily predict where you're headed in life, good or bad. They are what you repeatedly do and who you ultimately become. In essence, habits are the foundation for your success or failure.

Bad habits lead to failure, loss, debt, poor health, obesity, addictions, missed opportunities, failed relationships, and a host of other problems. Once you learn the importance of changing your daily patterns, this skill will be useful in overcoming eating disorders, addictions, procrastination, laziness, and unconscious habits that are holding you back.

When you look at a person you admire for the success they have attained, what you don't see are the hours, days, months and years they have routinely performed the *same* behavior day-in and day-out with nobody watching. From entrepreneurs to authors, celebrities and ministers, nearly 100% will attribute their success to the daily disciplines they've adapted in their lives. These seemingly small, behavioral adjustments lead to long-term results.

A *habit* is defined as "a recurring pattern of behavior or a series of repeated actions." It's not what you do once in a while that causes you to live an exceptional life; it's what you do consistently.

- 95% of those who lose weight will regain their weight loss.

Why? Habits.

- 30% of those who set New Year's goals quit the first week. Why? Habits.

- 80% of those who win the lottery file bankruptcy within five years! Why? Habits.

If you're ready to take your life to the next level and you're wondering why you haven't achieved the dreams that are in your heart, it could boil down to what you're doing at the break of dawn.

Aristotle said, "95% of everything you do is the result of habit."

We are creatures of habit! Research indicates that you wear 20% of your clothes 80% of the time. You go to the same restaurants and order the same things. You brush your teeth the same way every day. You put mascara on the same way. You put your socks and shoes on the same way. You take your vitamins, make your coffee, drive to work, park in the same spot, greet your coworkers and check your emails the same way day-in and day-out.

The problem with being habitual is that the habits you currently have are only good enough to get you what you have currently got! To go higher, achieve greater, and earn more, you will have to get some new habits!

Keystone Habits

We are bombarded by commercials tempting us with age-defying, waist-reducing, wealth-producing products without any indication of the effort, dedication, self-discipline, and time it will take to achieve it. Success comes through hard work. There is no shortcut or easy path to get to your dreams. Success is a marathon, not a sprint.

"I want it, and I want it now" is the cry of the undisciplined and unsuccessful. And that's why developing good habits is so difficult for them. Habits imply a lifestyle; not a temporary experiment.

How do you develop a new habit? By repetition.

> **"Success is the sum of small efforts,**
> **repeated day in and day out."**
> **- Robert Collier**

You will notice in this chapter that none of the five habits demand a major life overhaul. Instead, it's about making small tweaks and adjustments to your daily agenda that lead to stellar results. After researching and observing the common habits of ultra successful people, I have been amazed to discover that these general habits are the same ones I began practicing in 2002. Although, there are dozens more that contribute to their overall success, these five, in particular, are foundational for adapting other positive habits.

Charles Duhigg, bestselling author of *The Power of Habit*, calls them keystone habits.[17] A keystone habit is one that leads to developing other good habits. In other words, one keystone habit starts a chain effect that produces a list of positive behaviors.

For example, let's say your keystone habit is to sleep at least 7-8 hours every night. Your goal is to practice getting more rest, but this initial habit leads to other positive, unexpected results such as:

- Less time wasted watching television each night because you go to bed earlier.
- Exercising each morning because you have more energy.
- Becoming more productive in the morning because you're well-rested.
- Being more pleasant to be around because you're not cranky.

And you thought you were just aiming to get some sleep.

These keystone habits are a vital part of your personal growth. I never knew that's what I was forming back in 2002 when I made my list of five things to do each day. But these five keystone habits produced a trickle-down effect impacting every area of my life.

You don't have to make a list of a dozen habits to reach your goals. When you change a handful of these building block behaviors, it will impact your entire lifestyle. Small changes that you introduce into your routine will unexpectedly carry over into other aspects of your life. It truly is remarkable!

5 Things Successful People Do Before 8:00 A.M.

Let me introduce you to the five habits of success that transformed my personal routine and life. There is so much I want to share with you about each habit, so I will briefly introduce them to you here. Then I will dedicate an entire chapter to each habit.

MY DAILY ROUTINE

Gigi Butler
Founder of Gigi's Cupcakes
Daily 5:

1. I start with a prayer of thanksgiving for having another day.

2. I take my vitamins and eat a healthy breakfast.

3. Working out or walking really keeps my stress level down and it makes me have more energy and feel better about myself.

4. I have a list of goals I would like to accomplish that day and check them off. They could be as simple as "wash the dog" or "water the plants". When I have a list and can check them off, it gives me a sense of accomplishment.

5. I read Psalms and Proverbs every day. Even a single verse will center my soul and start my day off right. These two books are chock-full of wisdom.

1. They pray/meditate.

No matter what religion they are affiliated with, successful people make prayer/meditation a top priority in their day. People from all religions, backgrounds, and careers have discovered this "success habit" as a form of helping them relax, unwind, and improve their personal lives.

Doctors even prescribe meditation to lower stress levels and help with pain management. "Science has shown that it may even improve memory and brain function," said Benjamin Neal. "It's being taught in schools, to help kids focus and learn in the classroom. It's used by actors, artists, and innovators as a way to boost creativity and get in the zone."[18]

Actors Jennifer Aniston, Kristen Bell, Tom Hanks, Hugh Jackman, and Cameron Diaz (to name a few) find meditation helpful. Supermodel Gisele Bundchen, singers Sheryl Crow, Paul McCartney and Katy Perry, Comedians Ellen DeGeneres, Jerry Seinfeld, and Steve Harvey, authors Tim Ferris, Tony Robbins, and many more use meditation as a part of their daily ritual to prepare them for the day.

Oprah Winfrey, who went from extreme poverty to becoming one of the wealthiest women in the world, spends at least 20 minutes once or twice a day meditating. "Only from that space," she says, "can you create your best work, and your best life."[19]

> **"One of the things—and this comes from someone who was highly self-critical and a type-A personality—that has changed my life is meditating."**
> **- Sheryl Crow**

I am not endorsing or condoning all types of meditation as a habit you should incorporate. I am simply pointing out that these highly successful celebrities have tapped into a habit that comes from the

Word of God, even if they don't realize it. Prayer and meditation of God's Word is a solution for success prescribed by God Himself.

Now, people from all walks of life find the habit of getting still and quieting the noise around them as key in helping them get centered, focused, and relaxed before they begin the day. Some recommend focusing on the Universe; however, I communicate with the Creator of the Universe. I am only endorsing praying and meditation with the One true God and His Word, *The Holy Bible*, which is our manual for success.

"Keep this Book of the Law always on your lips; *meditate* on it day and night, so that you may be careful to do everything written in it. Then you will be prosperous and successful" (Joshua 1:8, NIV emphasis added).

So, according to God, you have to meditate on His Word if you want to be successful. Meditation isn't just for monks or hippies; it is a necessary part of the Christian life. Prayer is simply talking to God. It is our direct line to Heaven. Meditation is listening for God. It is where we sit quietly and direct our thinking on Him and His Word.

In Chapter 3, I will help you develop a habit of prayer and meditation as a keystone habit that will lead to a series of other life-changing patterns of behavior.

I don't use the words life-changing haphazardly. This single habit of prayer and meditation is the forerunner for all others. It is the one you need more than any other habit. If you just incorporate this one, primary change in your routine, it will dramatically affect everything in your life.

This is the cornerstone of success. Prayer and meditation is where you can experience relationships restored, receive God-inspired ideas that produce streams of revenue in your life, obtain energy in your body to go after the other habits, develop a sense of appreciation for where you currently are in life, gain strength to make it through any trial or challenge you're facing, and hear God's voice more clearly than ever before.

2. They read. (A lot!)

**"Your life will be determined over the
next 5 years by the people you hang
around and the books you read."
- Jim Rohn**

Do you know what you are most likely to find by a wealthy person's nightstand? Well, if you're from Texas, it could be a gun, but in most cases it's books. In fact, they discovered the largest homes of the wealthiest people had something in common that lower income homes do not have: a library.

Leaders are readers. The old adage that you must "learn more to earn more" is still true today. Wealthy, successful people approach a $30 book as though it has the potential to make them millions of dollars. I read where (did you notice that I read) Bill Gates and Warren Buffet were asked if they could have any superpower what would it be? Keep in mind that these two men are in the top five of the wealthiest people in the world. They realize that this superpower could get them anything they wanted in life. They both responded that they would want to be able to "read super fast"![20] The proof is in the pudding!

One major K.E.Y. to success is Keep Educating Yourself.

Actor Ashton Kutcher said, "The sexiest thing in the entire world is being smart, and being thoughtful, and being generous."[21] Success is tied to your personal development. You can't grow any more if you don't learn anymore. This is something I had to force myself to do because reading was always an obligation not an opportunity in my mind. In chapter 4, I will walk you through how and why my view on reading changed.

Remember, you have to change your mindset from viewing growth as a period of life to a way of life. According to Jim Rohn, "What a man reads pours massive ingredients into his mental factory and the fabric of his life is built from those ingredients." The Bible says, "As (a man) thinketh in his heart, so is he" (Proverbs 23:7, KJV).

Bishop TD Jakes says, "I ought to be able to look in your surroundings and know your dream." Jakes continues, "Are the books you're reading taking you to your dream? Are the seminars you're attending taking you to your dream? Is what you're doing in private taking you to your dream? Is where you're spending your money taking you closer to your dream? Show me your checking account and I'll show you your priorities."[22]

This is another keystone habit in which other great habits will emerge. Opportunities will open as your mind opens. Ideas will flourish as you turn the pages of a book. And it begins by building your personal library.

3. They listen to audio teaching.

This is the easiest of all the habits to adapt in your life. It only requires two words and very little physical effort: Push play! As we discovered in Habit #2, successful people read each morning, but they also take advantage of every available means to increase their knowledge by listening to audio teaching. Whether that includes during their jog or their commute to the office, they grow as they go.

> "The person who stops studying
> merely because he has finished
> school is forever hopelessly doomed
> to mediocrity, no matter what their
> calling."
> - Napoleon Hill

In our busy world where time is the most valuable commodity we have, many do not have an hour each day to simply read a book (or three hours like Mark Cuban[23]). But we do have time to listen. With this habit, you don't need to stop everything you're doing to commit to it, you can simply incorporate it with your current activities.

Beyond establishing just any good habit, this tradition changed my entire mindset. The Bible says that "faith comes by hearing, and hearing by the word of God" (Romans 10:17, NKJV). Every time you hear God's Word through a faith-building, motivational message, faith comes. *Faith* is defined as "trust or confidence." My trust in God grew, and my confidence dramatically increased.

When you add this habit to your drive time ritual, you can literally learn everything from marketing and business to finance and leadership, nutrition advice and spiritual guidance, as well as learning a foreign language all behind the steering wheel. You can go to college in your car while running errands, shopping, picking up the kids, waiting in traffic, and driving to work each way.

4. They write (and review) their dreams and goals.

> **"It is only a dream until you write it down, then it is a goal."**
> **- Emmitt Smith**

This is why 3% of the Harvard graduates in 1979 made 10 times as much as the other 97% combined! If you're familiar with this famous research, it shows the powerful effect of goal-setting and specifically, writing your goals, to contribute to your overall success.

Psychology professor at Dominican University, Dr. Gail Matthews conducted a similar study on goal-setting using 267 participants. She found that you are 42% more likely to achieve your goals just by writing them down.[24]

Writing your dreams and goals is a clear key to success!

Everyone seems to agree on the importance that goals should be written down; however, only 3 out of every 100 adults write their goals on paper. The act of penning your aspirations on paper is a powerful motivator. It forces you to get specific about your ambitions. Tony Robbins says, "Setting goals is the first step in turning the invisible into the visible."

As we study this further in Chapter 6, you'll see the ripple effect this keystone habit has on your life. If you have a goal of weighing a certain amount, it will affect your exercise and nutrition habits. If you have a goal of owning a business, it will affect your reading and networking habits. If you have a goal of being debt-free, it will affect your spending and budgeting habits.

The world's most successful people agree that what you get by achieving your goals isn't nearly as important as who you *become* in the process.

5. They exercise.

It's no surprise that physical fitness and success go hand in hand. The most successful people consider exercise integral to their overall achievements in life. They know that working out consistently is the key to mental and physical health. It is one of the most important habits you should develop to transform your life and live your dreams.

In addition to losing weight and improving your overall physical appearance, this ritual alone can build your self-esteem, reduce stress, improve sleep, boost your memory and concentration, and consequently make you happier. Even knowing all these rewarding benefits, CBS reported that 80% of Americans adults don't get enough exercise.[25]

As a rule, when you start exercising habitually, you start changing other patterns in your life. Traditionally, people begin eating healthier foods, drinking more water, smoking and/or drinking less, and even spending less money on eating fast food. Not only is exercise considered a keystone habit, but researchers have even said that something about it that makes other good habits easier.[26]

Inc.com reported that 70% of successful business individuals discover a way to exercise each day. They know they need energy to get ahead, and the best way to have that is to eat healthier, exercise and get proper rest.

In Chapter 7, I'm going to show you how to make exercise a part of your lifestyle in a simple, beneficial way. It will become like brushing your teeth. You will no longer make your decision based on how you feel, you just do it. This is not necessarily about being bikini ready (unless that's your goal) or competing on stage for Mrs. Universe. It's about getting in shape, inside and out, to be fit for your life assignment. It's about creating routines in your life that bring about the best you imaginable.

Change Your Routine, Change Your Life

So, the early bird does, in fact, catch the worm. When I joined the ranks of early-risers and established those five simple habits, I never dreamed something so unspectacular would enable me to stand before Presidents, launch books in several languages, and stand onstage in arenas of thousands of people simply sharing the secret of my success.

Today, when people (like the woman in the introduction) ask me, "How did you get a life like this?" I simply say, "My routine."

- I stopped rolling over...and started rolling out at 5 a.m.
- I stopped making excuses...and started making time to pray.
- I stopped scrolling through Facebook...and started reading books.
- I stopped listening to fear...and started listening to faith-building, motivational messages.

- I stopped keeping up with the Kardashians...and started keeping my commitment at the gym.
- I changed my routine, and it changed my life.

Now that you know the five habits you need to start, let's dig deeper into the first pivotal habit that explains why successful people spend time alone.

MY DAILY ROUTINE

Lisa Osteen Comes
Associate Pastor of Lakewood Church, author
Daily 5:

1. I read my Bible, pray, worship, and make positive declarations over my life the first 30 minutes in the morning.

2. I write in my gratitude journal.

3. I do Pilates and walk for exercise.

4. I eat healthy meals. This recent change has given me more energy and I simply feel better.

5. I laugh and have fun EVERY day (even on the stressful days)!

3

WHY SUCCESSFUL PEOPLE SPEND TIME ALONE

HABIT #1: PRAY AND MEDITATE

'll never forget that first morning I began this habit of aloneness. After dropping my little girl off at school, I drove home, walked into my den, grabbed a journal and pen, and just sat there. The stillness of the room was a frightening sound to me. It annoyed me to not have background noise. The TV, music, someone on the phone, the neighbor mowing their lawn, the garbage truck collecting bins, birds chirping. Seriously anything rather than quietness.

I had no idea that I was afraid of my own thoughts. I was scared to think about how messed up my life had become. I didn't want to be honest with myself or with God about how confused I was or how disappointed I felt with where I had ended up in life. Being alone proved to be the absolute best thing that could have ever happened to me.

What started out as near torture turned into pure delight. This morning routine of sitting quietly, journaling my thoughts, and listening for that still, small voice from God, brought more healing to my heart than any counselor's advice or any quotes from a bestselling book. It is *the* reason I am doing what I'm doing today.

If you choose to start your morning routine with only one, single habit, this is the one that will alter the course of your life for the better in every way. It doesn't require participation from anyone else other than you. Solitude is the most important part of pursuing God's dream for your life. This is where you gain direction, obtain clarity for your vision, receive courage to overcome obstacles, and become fearless in the face of adversity to go after your dreams. There is strength in solitude.

For years now, I've kept a journal from my quiet times to plan my dreams and goals, and to develop strategies to help me achieve them. The rewards of spending time alone to journal your thoughts and prayers are endless. God is the One who said that He is a "rewarder of those who diligently seek Him" (Hebrews 11:6, NKJV).

Warning: This habit of stillness is the most convenient one to neglect (even more than exercise). Getting away from all the distractions vying for your attention will be the most challenging habit to acquire, but the greatest discipline you can obtain.

The average person spends their day with so much noise. We start our mornings checking our social media posts before we even get dressed for the day. We have the radio or the news on in the background while we're getting ready. We jam out to our favorite songs on the way to work. We spend our workdays listening to co-workers. We come home and get caught up with who won the latest dance routine, got kicked off the island or who's mad at what's happening in the White House again. Until it's time to go to bed and start the process over again. We spend most of our time listening to other voices and rarely our own, much less the voice of God.

How often do you hear nothing? When was the last time you sat quietly in a room by yourself and just thought? "About what, Terri," you may ask. About life. Your future. Where you're headed. Where you see yourself five years from now. What you really want. What you want to change. What's bothering you. Who you need to forgive. What you need to stop. What you need to start. What God is speaking to your heart. Perhaps, like me, you haven't gotten still enough to ask yourself those vital questions or more importantly, to obtain answers.

In the Bible, most people got their vision out in the hills, the deserts, the wilderness, in the quiet place of solitude. Jesus went off alone. Paul spent time alone. Moses spent time alone. Alone is where you receive direction, clarity, answers, wisdom, and confidence.

God wants to give you the direction you so desperately desire. He wants to reveal His next steps for your life and even give you those God-inspired ideas that produce great wealth. He wants to whisper insights and creative concepts, but you must get quiet to hear them. Prayer is you talking—meditation is you listening!

For some people, the word *meditate* is a bad word. They associate it with New Age religions or other things they find strange. Of course there are many types of meditation, but I'm referring to a believer's devotional life. The Bible uses the word *meditate* 29 times in the *New International Version*. God wants you to meditate. He even explains that meditation is a part of your journey to success, Joshua 1:8 says, "Keep this Book of the Law always on your lips; meditate on it day and night, so that you may be careful to do everything written in it. Then you will be prosperous and successful" (NIV).

According to God, you have to meditate on His Word if you want to be successful. Meditation is the most important aspect of prayer. Most people never meditate. They talk too much in prayer. You never hear from God while you're talking. Most people tell the Lord what's on their hearts, plead for things, then their prayer is over. Your dream is never revealed to you while you're talking. You have to be quiet and listen. When you do, you'll be amazed how loud He speaks.

Hidden Wisdom

An ancient legend tells of a time when ordinary people had access to all the knowledge of the gods. Yet time and again, they ignored this wisdom. Finally, the gods grew tired of so freely giving a gift the people didn't value or utilize, so they decided to hide this precious wisdom where only the most committed of seekers would discover it. They believed that if people had to work hard to find wisdom, they would use it more carefully.

One of the gods suggested that they bury it deep in the earth. "No," the others said, "too many people could easily dig down and find it."

"Let's put it in the deepest ocean," suggested one of the gods, but that idea was also rejected. They knew that people would one day learn to dive and thus would find it too easily.

One of the gods suggested hiding it on the highest mountaintop, but it was quickly agreed that people could climb mountains.

Finally, one of the wisest gods suggested, "Let's hide it deep inside the people themselves. They'll never think to look in there." And so it came to be—and so it continues today.[27]

Don't freak out on me! I'm not suggesting this legend is true. What am I saying? You have the *wisdom of God* already on the inside of you, but you have to get still and listen for it! This is where you envision your future. This is where you receive clarity for your life. As a leader, this is the most valuable thing you can do for your organization. Give your team the direction that you receive in prayer. As a spouse or parent, it's the most valuable thing you can do for your family. As an individual, it's the most valuable thing you can do for your life.

Wisdom in the Quiet

In 1984, Madeline Balletta was praying for a solution to her fatigue and intense back pain. Being a Christian and knowing that God speaks to His children in a still, small voice, one day in prayer she heard the unusual words: fresh royal jelly.

Not understanding the meaning behind this unique directive, she did some research. In her discovery, she found that royal jelly was the actual food substance worker bees fed to the queen in their hives. It is a pure, natural, highly nourishing liquid that was beginning distribution in England as a nutritional supplement. Madeline began using it and seeing drastic improvement with her energy and overall well-being.

Consequently, she began to ask the Lord if royal jelly was meant to do more than only help her. "Start a company" were the words she heard in her quiet time with God. So, she obeyed. Today, her company, Bee-Alive, went from words on the pages of a journal, to an experiment in her garage, to a multimillion dollar company!

To this day, Madeline seeks the Lord for wisdom, clarity, and direction for her life and He always provides it. She isn't shy about sharing where it all came from. "I believe God gave me the vision, the inspiration, the strength, and the courage to see it all through." Madeline says.[28]

Think about it. Because Madeline Balletta took the time to get away from all the distractions, to sit quietly, and listen for God-inspired wisdom and ideas, she not only changed the entire trajectory of her life but also provided an amazing lifestyle for her children and grandchildren, not to mention those who have benefitted from her company.

Super-Thinking

Great leaders spend time alone listening for that still, small voice. We usually imagine successful people busy networking with others most of the time, and yes, a great portion of time is spent interacting with teams and networking, but successful people spend considerable time alone thinking, listening and journaling their thoughts and their time in prayer.

In the bestselling book, *The Magic of Thinking Big*, David Schwartz says, "Successful people in any field take time out to confer with (themselves). Leaders use solitude to put the pieces of the problem together to work out solutions, to plan and in one phrase, to do their super-thinking. Many people fail to tap their creative leadership power because they confer with everybody and everything else but themselves." Look at these political leaders who made lasting names for themselves in history—good or bad—by gaining insight in their alone time.

- Franklin D. Roosevelt capitalized on his time alone while recovering from his polio attack.
- Harry Truman spent time alone on a Missouri farm.
- Adolf Hitler spent months in jail alone where he had time to construct a wicked plan for world conquest.
- Communist leaders, Lenin, Stalin, Marx and others spent time in jail where they planned their future moves.
- Thomas Edison said, "My best thinking has been done in solitude."[29]

John Maxwell says, "It doesn't matter what profession a person pursues, thinking precedes achievement. Success doesn't come by accident. People don't repeatedly stumble into achievement and then figure it out afterward. The greater your thinking, the greater your potential."

To *think* means "to imagine, to concentrate, to focus, to center your attention, to meditate." To *meditate* means "to chew over, to ponder, to reflect, to mull over." Claude M. Bristol, bestselling author of *The Magic of Believing*, said, "Thought is the original source of all wealth, all success, all material gain, all great discoveries and inventions, and all achievement."[30]

Chick-fil-A CEO, Dan Cathy, admits to spending half a day every two weeks and one solid day each month completely alone. He allocates 15-20 minutes in solitude before starting each day. Arianna Huffington, of *The Huffington Post*, begins each day with 30 minutes of meditation claiming that it calms her mind and helps her focus. Actor Will Arnett admits to writing down 10 things he's grateful for every morning. Steve Harvey looks forward to waking up saying, "When I wake up in the morning, I spend the first 10 minutes thanking Him. I don't even address any problems and stuff I've got. I'm grateful that I'm up for this. It makes your day start such a wonderful way."

Jesus spent time alone in prayer. If that was the only example I gave you, it would be enough. If Jesus did it, I want to do it too.

We need these consistent times in solitude. You might be asking, "But what do I do when I'm alone?" You will need two items, and they will prove to be the greatest tools on your journey to success. A journal and a pen.

Keep a Journal

**"A life worth living is a life
worth recording."
- Jim Rohn**

Keeping a journal isn't just for teenage girls documenting every move of their crush at school. It's for business leaders, presidents, authors, entrepreneurs and dream achievers. A journal not only gives you a place to record your thoughts, but it allows you to analyze where you've been, where you are, and where you are headed. Journals are not for recording what you ate for breakfast or what you wore to class yesterday. Don't mistake this for a diary of your daily activities.

So what do you journal? When you hear something valuable, write it down. When you stumble across something important, meaningful, or inspiring, write it down. When you feel God is speaking to you in prayer, write it down. When you need clarity and direction for your life, write it down. Don't count on your memory to remember it all. Write it down.

Where do you think I've gotten all the quotes in my books from? I certainly didn't memorize them all. I have collected them in my journals as I have read them over years.

The late Jim Rohn "used to take notes on pieces of paper and torn-off corners and backs of old envelopes…and pieces of paper thrown in a drawer. Then I found out that the best way to organize those ideas is to keep a journal…The discipline makes up a valuable part of my learning, and the journals are a valuable part of my library."[31]

Many famous people from all walks of life kept journals: businessman John D. Rockefeller; military great George Patton; inventors Ben Franklin and Thomas Edison; presidents John Adams, Ronald Reagan and prime minister Winston Churchill; authors Mark Twain and Ernest Hemingway, etc. Their journals became pieces of the legacy they left behind.

The list of reasons and benefits of keeping a journal is endless. I have heard of journaling doing everything from improving your mental health to reducing stress, from eliminating anxiety to boosting energy. For me, it has provided crystal clear direction for my life and ministry.

You will never look at buying a journal the same way after you hear more of Jim Rohn's point of view: "I am a buyer of blank books…The reason I pay $26 (for a journal) is to challenge myself to find something worth $26 to put in there…If you ever got a hold of one of them, you wouldn't have to look very far to discover it is worth more than $26."[32]

I love that! Make the content of your journal worth more than the price you paid for it. After all, it's pretty much your autobiography.

Let's look at five of the most powerful reasons to keep a journal.

1. Record your ideas.

Many of us have a great idea but before we ever think to write it down, it's gone. Even in the business world, success coaches advise their associates to immediately capture their thoughts and ideas in writing as soon as possible. Research indicates that any new ideas not captured *within 37 seconds* are likely never to be recalled again. After 7 minutes, it's gone forever![33]

Life coach Stacia Pierce said, "Once the words and images hit the paper, you have now crystallized a thought or idea. You can use the power of pen and paper to strategize and create anything you want."[34]

The quality of your thinking has the greatest consequences of all! In 2013, I set a goal to make myself sit quietly for 20 minutes one day a week. So 52 times that year, I sat quietly for 20 minutes and wrote whatever I heard in my spirit. I came across that journal recently, and I began reading some of those private entries the other day. It was verbatim what is happening in my life right now! I was stunned to see the accuracy of what I felt God was revealing to me and what my current reality is. The words on those pages and my life today were one and the same.

Ideas are all around you. Creative ideas will come to you at the most random times. Documenting these ideas in your journal could provide a solution to your breakthrough. Getting your ideas on paper ensures you have it recorded, and now, you can start developing plans to put those ideas into action.

"As soon as you think it, ink it!"
- Mark Victor Hansen

2. Identify your thoughts.

Writing in a journal can help you express your emotions. It becomes a tool for self-improvement. You truly get to know yourself more when you pinpoint your thoughts and feelings in writing. You'll be able to identify what is holding you back, what you're struggling to overcome, and the reasons behind your decisions.

This little journal is a safe space where you get to be honest with yourself. It's so important that you don't write with the intent of someone reading it. This is your personal journey, your story. It's intimate to you and you get to reveal yourself with no restraints about who you really are and what you truly want.

Keeping a journal literally empties your brain of all the thoughts going through your head at any given time. When you need to make big decisions for your life—where to move, which job to take, who to marry, where to apply, when to open your business, which university to attend, which offer to accept—getting your thoughts out of your head and onto paper helps you make better decisions. Journaling has been shown to improve emotional health, mental health, and even reduce stress which improves your physical health.

When I first began journaling my thoughts, I was shocked. The more I wrote, the more sincere and honest I was about my feelings at that time. Why was my marriage falling apart? What led me to making poor decisions that resulted in this miserable state of mind? Why was I angry? What had caused so much hurt? Why did I hide my feelings even from those I loved the most? Why was I insecure and feeling inferior? The more I penned my thoughts, the deeper I dove into my reality.

I found healing on the pages of those journals. I wrote out scriptures that brought peace to my tormented mind. I realized as I read over my previous weeks of journaling that I was so focused on all the negativity in my life that it was blocking me from seeing anything positive. This forced me to begin identifying things to be grateful for. It's almost as if you become your own counselor when you write your thoughts.

Today, my journals are more about direction for my life. As my thoughts are documented on the pages, I notice where I still need to overcome fears or anxieties, where I need to grow, where to invest my time better, and where I need to sit still more and hear from God.

You hear people say, "Don't just sit there; do something!" I always say, "Don't just do something; sit there...and listen. Then write it in your journal."

3. Find clarity.

Clarity comes from questions. When you sit quietly and ask yourself tough questions, you gain a new understanding as you write your responses. You don't have to edit yourself or impress anyone. Just let the words flow and clarity will come.

Not too long ago, I felt so uneasy inside. I was stressed out, overworked and feeling pretty miserable with my current schedule. Finally, I took my own advice and I sat quietly with my journal. I began asking myself pointed questions concerning my state of mind, and I was able to identify my solution. Each question compelled me to dig deeper to find the answer and ultimately pointed me in a new direction. Had I not journaled that experience, I would still be running in circles wondering why I was exhausted.

Even the Bible tells us to ask for clarity. "If any of you lacks wisdom, let him ask," (James 1:5, NKJV).

If you lack clarity and direction in some aspect of your life or you are feeling stress in your current situation, ask yourself these questions. Ask God for wisdom and then write out your answers:

- What advice would you give to someone in your situation?
- What do you want to do?
- What would make the situation better?
- What actions do you need to take to change things?
- What are you doing wrong?
- What are you doing right?

With distractions all around you, the best thing you can do is sit down, get out your journal and ask questions. If you're hazy about an issue in your life, write it out. This will help you make tough decisions. Instead of keeping those thoughts going in circles in your head, pen them on paper. Start listing consequences of each decision. What are the pros and cons? List every possible outcome of the choice you need to make. Research supports that writing your thoughts versus talking about them produces greater levels of peace, confidence, self-esteem, and happiness.

4. Plan your future.

My journal is where I began getting honest with myself about my future. I'll explain much more about this vital habit in Chapter 7. As you sit quietly and create your ideal life on paper, it is like programming the GPS in your car and giving yourself a clear map to follow.

Your journal is your personal space to ponder and pen your aspirations. It's where you answer questions about where you want to live, what you want to have, how you want to be remembered, how much money you want to save, what you want to become, who you want to meet or work with, etc. These questions help you identify your true desires. Once answered, the pages inside this little journal will become your road map for success.

In an interview with Oprah, Fergie, the lead singer for The Black Eyed Peas, shared some of the steps she took to overcome her drug addiction to Crystal Meth. As simple as it seems, she had a journal and a pen as part of her therapy and recovery. In the pages of her journal, she began to "figure herself out," but also got crystal clear about her future. She got honest with herself as she wrote page after page about what she wanted to achieve.

She wanted to have a solo album with a number one song. She wanted to win a Grammy. She wanted to overcome feelings of guilt and unworthiness from her negative experiences. She learned how to quiet the self-doubt, believe in herself, and get in touch with her true desires...all within the pages of a simple journal. Never underestimate the power of a blank book. Today, Fergie has won eight Grammys and her debut solo album, "The Dutchess," received three number one hit singles. I would say that today her journal is worth more than the price tag on the back cover of a blank book.[35]

It's in these quiet times that you truly get honest with yourself. Like any habit, the more you practice it, the more comfortable you get doing it. It will become something you desire doing as you realize the impact it has on every aspect of your life.

5. Hear from the Lord in prayer.

My dad taught me years ago to always take a journal and a pen into my quiet times with the Lord to practice hearing the voice of God. The Bible says, "My sheep hear my voice" (John 10:27, NKJV). God expects you to hear from Him. It's not strange. It's not mystical. It's not creepy. It's quite the opposite. It provides clarity, confidence, peace, comfort, direction, and wisdom for your life.

Admittedly, I've never heard an audible voice in prayer. What you hear is more like an impression on the inside. My dad always told me, "Whatever comes up in your spirit, write it down." Many times I've wondered, "Is that God or just my own head making this up?" But I started writing it down anyway. This single practice of journaling my prayer time has provided more direction for my life than any other habit. No exaggeration.

Starting your day in prayer is what sets the tone for the day. We can have devotionals, go to church, listen to messages, but *nothing* takes the place of quality time with God.

God even instructed us to journal His words to us. "Thus says the Lord God of Israel, 'Write in a book all the words which I have spoken to you" (Jeremiah 30:2, AMP). Why? Again, because we forget.

Warning: if you've never journaled your thoughts before or ever practiced hearing from the Lord, you will have to fight the doubts in your head convincing you that God won't speak to you. That is a lie. God wants you to hear His voice more than anything. Don't over-think your writing. Don't allow doubt to stop you from writing what you hear inside. Just start and write whatever enters your mind. Your journal is not intended to be a polished article. These are simply your thoughts and impressions from the Lord.

Practical Tips for Hearing from God

Create the right atmosphere in your home.

A cluttered environment is the sign of a cluttered mind. If your surroundings are out of order, your life may be out of order. It is so important that you designate a room in your house that brings the most peace to you, and make that your room, your spot, your special place to get quiet. If you go into a room desiring to hear from God and that space is disorganized, junky or cluttered, you're most likely going to focus more on what needs to be cleaned than hearing from the Lord.

MY DAILY ROUTINE

Dee Dee Freeman
Wife, mom, minister
Daily 5:

1. Seek God first and ask Him what He wants me to do today. It may change my routine (Matthew 6:33).

2. Pray in the Spirit.

3. Pray with my understanding. I ask God to expose, reveal,

and remove anything and anyone that does not have my best interest at heart today (and to replace it or them).

4. Study God's Word.

5. Identify someone to bless by my words, presence, or resources.

T. L. Osborne said, "Tranquility produces creativity." Clean up your surroundings. Create a space that welcomes the Holy Spirit, that brings peace to your mind, and removes anything competing for your attention.

My dad says to imagine the Holy Ghost as a holy guest in your home. How would you want your room to look if someone you considered a holy guest were to walk in? In other words, if you knew someone like Joyce Meyer, Joel Osteen, or Jerry Savelle were coming to your house today, how would you want to present that room? In what condition would it need to be for you to not feel embarrassed, ashamed, or humiliated with its appearance? Whatever your answer is to that question, get it show ready.

Recently, I was speaking at a conference in Denver, Colorado and when I walked in the speaker's room, I gasped! It was my first introduction to the host who invited me, and I was shocked at how well she knew my style, my taste, and my *favorite* everything. Everywhere I looked, she had creatively placed little displays of Terri. On one table sat a gorgeous vase of freshly bloomed pink roses. Another table was scattered with miniature Eiffel Towers and dozens of mouth-watering cupcakes piled high with pink, buttercream icing. Several copies of my books were enlarged and displayed on the stage. Wallpaper was printed and covering the doors into the sanctuary, the restrooms, and the exit doors displaying picturesque scenes of the City of Lights (Paris, France). French music was playing in the hospitality room, and some women were even wearing French couture. I was overwhelmed at their hospitality and their detailed preparation for my arrival. I felt so welcomed.

You can produce the same preparation with your Heavenly Father. Create an atmosphere that reveals your preparation for His arrival, that causes Him to feel welcome and that is conducive for Him to speak into your life.

Create the right atmosphere in your heart.

In addition to clearing the clutter in your surroundings, you may need to empty out the junk from your past. When we hold on to debilitating emotions and experiences—unforgiveness, sin, strife, anger, bitterness, shame, guilt—it blocks our ability to hear from God. This could be the reason you feel as if there's a wall between you and God, and you can't hear Him clearly.

Have you ever walked into someone's house and you knew there had been a fight? You didn't hear the argument, you didn't see the dishes flying, you didn't witness the uproar, but somehow you could sense an awkwardness in the atmosphere? What are you inclined to do in a situation like that? Get out as soon as possible! The house may look like a museum on the outside, but the spiritual atmosphere stinks on the inside!

Well, the Holy Spirit is just as uncomfortable in an unclean, strife-filled heart. The simple solution to decluttering your heart is to repent. Get free from anything that's separating you from God. All you need to do is ask the Lord to forgive you for anything that displeased Him and brought shame or guilt into your life. Here's the good news: God forgives you the first time you ask. His forgiveness is instant, and it opens the door for Him to walk right in and feel at home in your presence.

Look what Isaiah said when he sensed his sin (uncleanness) in God's presence, "Woe to me! I am ruined! For I am a man of unclean lips, and

I live among a people of unclean lips, and my eyes have seen the King, the Lord Almighty" (Isaiah 6:5, NIV).

He immediately sensed his uncleanness in God's presence. The scripture goes on to explain that an angel touched his lips and his guilt was taken away. I love what the next verse says: "Then I heard the voice of the Lord..." (verse 8).

After he was cleansed of his sin, he heard the Lord speak. You may have experiences from your past that are still tormenting your mind; maybe you've never come before God and repented. Ask Him to forgive you right now. Don't go another day with that clutter on the inside of you.

James 4:8 says, "Draw near unto God and He will draw near unto you" (NASB). In other words, you make the first move. God is such a gentleman that He waits for you to take the first step. Take a step closer to God, and He'll take one closer to you.

Write whatever you hear.

> **"Call to me and I will answer you,
> and show you great and mighty
> things..."
> - Jeremiah 33:3, NKJV**

Typically, whatever comes up in your heart is something God is dealing with you about.

You may even hear only one word: Forgive. Rest. Give. Stop. Freedom. Embrace. Discipline. One word heard from God can provide more direction for your life than an entire journal of random thoughts.

In fact, one year, I heard the word *invest*. So, I wrote it down. I researched the word *invest* and discovered it means "to allocate money (or sometimes another resource, such as time) in the expectation of some benefit in the future; to use, give, or devote (time, talent, etc.), for a purpose or to achieve something." All year that one single word became my decision maker. When an opportunity arose, I was constantly reminded to *invest*. I invested in relationships, in family, in education, in resources to learn, in finances, etc. Invest became my driving force all year long.

One Sunday that year, I was invited to attend a 25-year church anniversary service for some pastors who were longtime friends. It was quite a distance from my home, and it was my first weekend off in a long time. Even though I wanted to rest that day, using the word *invest* as my decision maker, I chose to invest my time to love on my friends.

Little did I know that God was setting me up to be extremely blessed! Before I left the church service to honor these precious pastors, they said, "Terri, we see what you're doing to impact lives in the nation of France and we want to give an offering into your missions outreach to the French people. Here's a check for $5,000!" What? *I went to honor them, and they blessed me*?! I went in obedience to my word from the Lord in prayer, and God honored it. Since then, those same pastors have sponsored our annual Icing Women's Event bringing young women in from safe houses and girls homes by donating $20,000! All because I allowed one word heard in prayer and scribbled in my journal to become my motivation for making decisions. God blessed it.

More and more of the same sort of experiences happened all year long because I focused in on one word I heard in prayer.

Another year, I heard a single word in prayer, and it was *purge*. That didn't sound appealing, so I looked it up and it means "to rid (someone) of an unwanted feeling, memory, or condition, typically giving a sense of release." I took it literally.

First, I wanted to be free from anything holding me back—my past, my old memories, guilt, shame, etc. Then, I looked at my schedule and purged the places where I was over-committed. I looked at purging my surroundings and started decluttering my house. I purged clothes, dresser drawers, movies, DVD's, books, dishes, etc. I even made over $5,000 selling stuff that was laying around my house.

Here's my point: after I got our home streamlined and in order, I had no idea that I would be purging myself from my job! That was the year God instructed me to resign my position as CEO and start my own ministry in a new city, new offices, new house, and start from scratch. But you know what? I was ready. Everything was purged and ready to go.

Another year, I heard the word *firm*. I felt the Lord instructing me to get firm in certain aspects of my life—not just my body parts but in my decision-making too! *Firm* means "fixed, stable, steady, difficult to disturb or move, solid, securely established, steadfast, unmovable, constant, unwavering, unyielding, resolute."

In my finances, I got firm about saving and investing money. I set up automatic withdrawals from my checking account into an investment account. I made a checklist of specific areas that I needed to get firm. In other words, I stopped talking about doing it one day and committed to doing it now. By the end of the year, they were done. That word forced me to follow through. I also went through some painful situations that year, and I had to remain firm, unmovable, unshakable in my faith, and that four-letter word kept me strong.

One single word heard in your quiet time can literally shape you, stretch you, and provide the direction you need all year long. It can laser-focus you on the key areas of your life. I highly recommend documenting in your journal every time you use this word in your decisions. Record it. You will see rapid growth in your life.

Pastor Craig Groeschel said one year he focused on the word *strengthen* and applied it to everything: his personal life, his ministry, his church, and his staff. He felt that his ministry was growing in numbers but not spiritually. People were getting trapped up in distractions, marriages were falling apart, students were falling into sin, small groups were having problems. He chose Isaiah 54:2 that says, "enlarge the place of your tent...*strengthen* your stakes" (NIV).

That one single word directed them all year long and as a result, marriages were strengthened, student ministries were overhauled and strengthened, and young people had revival. Groeschel's messages were focused around strengthening faith, families, relationships, finances, etc., and he reported, "Transformation took place in one year because of one word!"

Pastor Groeschel recently said that his new word for this year is *rest*. He wasn't happy about it. He wanted a powerful, ambitious word like *conquer* or *destroy*! He jokingly said, "If you don't like your word, it probably means God gave it to you."[36]

Make it a habit.

I want you to have this phrase memorized and ingrained in your thinking: The secret of your future is hidden in your daily routine.

What you do occasionally doesn't shape your life; it's what you do consistently. Set aside a certain time every day to listen, to think, and to write in your journal even if it's for five minutes.

Again, I prefer to start my morning with this habit because it clears my mind and sets the tone for the rest of the day. Assign a time each day that feels most comfortable with your routine. As you clear your mind, relax, and embrace this calm moment to be with the Lord. When you do, God promises in His Word that those who "dwell in the secret place of the most high God will remain stable..." (Psalm 91:1, AMPC). If your emotions feel unstable, here's your answer to stability: Connect with God. Invest time with Him. Listen for His voice.

Insight in Isolation

Successful people are committed to having "me-time" every single day.

They don't fear solitude; they embrace it. They schedule it. It's their moment to reflect, to recoup, to replenish their energy, and to relate with the Lord.

Just imagine a habit of hearing God-inspired ideas that produce a wealth of income. Imagine knowing which person to marry without hesitation, which deal to close without doubt, which project to launch without confusion. Imagine providing solutions in your company that bring significant promotion. Imagine being in the right places at the right times to make the right connections. This is why successful people spend time alone. There's great insight in isolation.

"Be still and know that I am God."
- Psalm 46:10, NIV

MY DAILY ROUTINE

Keith Craft
Lead Pastor of Elevate Life Church
Daily 5:

1. I start by making daily declarations...speaking over myself (This happens before my feet hit the floor...everyday, out loud)

2. I drink 32 ounces of water with a shot of organic lemon juice.

3. Take my morning vitamins.

4. 20 minutes of high intensity workout. I combine spirit, soul and body together and use this time to worship God with loud worship music. This establishes my rhythm for the day!

5. I read and meditate for one hour.

4

MOVE FORWARD
EACH DAY BY 1%

HABIT #2: READ

My graduation cap sat on top of my big, Texas-size hair, and my black robe was adorned with red tassels symbolizing my achievement of graduating *Cum Laude* from Texas Tech University. The day I had been counting down to for 52 months (I was on the 4.5-year plan!) had arrived. It was college graduation day.

"Terri Lynn Savelle, Bachelor of Arts," was my cue to walk across the stage in a coliseum of 7,000 people and receive my award for four years of studying the French language (my major) and learning how to communicate effectively (my minor). This was my moment of pay off! I put in the hours, I crammed for exams, and now I had the proof of my discipline to hang proudly on the wall.

A few hours later, the entire Savelle family joined up for our traditional Tex-Mex feast to celebrate my accomplishment at El Chico's in West Texas. As we ate the bottomless bowl of chips and salsa, I made a bold—yet idiotic—declaration to my family. "I will never study again!" I mean why would I? I had the degree. I graduated with honors. I was more educated than 70% of those who never finish college. I knew all I needed to know. It seemed good enough to last me *forever*. Ironically, that statement was proof of my ignorance.

The following statistics tell me there are probably a lot of people living like I used to:

- The number of non-book readers has nearly tripled since 1978.[37]
- 43% of U.S. adults do not read a book unless required by work or school.[38]
- 27% of U.S. adults have not read a book in the last 12 months.[39]

Announcing my ignorance to the family that day was probably the dumbest thing I have ever said. But what's worse is that it became the dumbest commitment I ever kept. I stood by that dumb promise of never studying for 11 years of my life! For more than a decade, I never picked up another book. I never listened to a motivational teaching (other than attending church on Sundays). I never invested in a conference. I never gleaned from a mentor, listened to an audiobook, or downloaded a podcast. Nothing. I pretty much *never studied again*! And my life proved it.

As I mentioned in the introduction of this book, I lived paycheck to paycheck. I paid my car note every month. I paid my credit cards faithfully. I had nothing in my savings account. I spent everything I earned. I woke up at the last minute to rush to the office and was the first to leave at 5:00 p.m. so I could hurry home and get enthralled in watching other people live their dreams (aka watching TV).

When I finally got desperate for change, I picked up one book and started with one page, one day at a time. Something surprising began to happen. The more I read, the more I wanted to learn. I was learning how to manage my time, how to reduce my debt, how to lead an organization, how to get my body in shape, how to organize my house, and how to set goals for my future. The more I learned, the more I began to earn. As a result, the next 11 years of my life, my income quadrupled, my cars were paid off, my savings account was healthy, and my investment portfolio was starting to grow. I went from proudly declaring I would never read to inspiring millions of people to build a personal library.

As I began to grow, everything around me grew. My life has seen enormous increase and success due to the information gleaned inside the pages of good books.

"The person who stops studying merely because they have finished school is forever hopelessly doomed to mediocrity, no matter what their calling."
- Napoleon Hill

For some reason, I had the mentality of reading books as an *obligation* rather than an *opportunity*. It was always an assignment I *had* to do, not something I *got* to do. I thought only nerdy people who lacked a good social life were the ones staying home on a Friday night curled up with a boring novel. I bet you've heard, "Be nice to nerds. Chances are you'll end up working for one."

Little did I realize that I was stuck in place at my current level of knowledge. I was still sharing information I learned in 1991 in the year 2001 because I hadn't grown in a decade.

Without fail, every single successful person I have studied has this one trait in common: They read, and they read a lot! In fact, 75% of self-made millionaires have reported to reading at least two books per month.[40] Unsuccessful people view growth as a *period* of life, as I did. Successful people view growth as a *way* of life. They never stop learning.

Most of the successful people you admire were not born into success. They simply did—and continue to do—things that help them tap into their full potential. And at the top of the list is reading.

If you desire to be a comedian, could you imagine getting to sit down with Steve Martin and learn everything he knows about stand-up comedy? You can. Steve tells it all in his autobiography *Born Standing Up: A Comic's Life.*

What about a dream to play tennis professionally? Why not be trained by Wimbledon (and US, French, and Australian Open) winner, tennis Hall of Famer Andre Agassi by reading his autobiography *Open.* You can be entertained in your kitchen for days with Julia Child's bestselling book, *The Art of French Cooking.* Or you can learn everything about running a business from the founder of the world's largest retailer, Walmart, Sam Walton, in his book, *Sam Walton: Made in America.* Why not learn how to tap into your full potential by reading Tony Robbins' classic, *Awaken the Giant Within?*

The opportunities to learn from the best are endless, and they are at your fingertips inside the pages of memoirs and study guides to success.

W. Clement Stone, the former publisher of *Success Magazine* who was worth $800 million, began to mentor young Jack Canfield in the early 1970's. During an interview with Jack, he wanted to get an idea of how much Jack valued personal development.

"I have a question for you," he asked Canfield. "Do you watch television?"

Canfield replied, "Yes, of course."

The mentor asked, "How many hours a day do you watch TV?"

"I don't know. I watch shows like *Good Morning, America.* The News. *Johnny Carson.* Maybe about three hours a day."

"Cut out one hour a day," said Stone.

Canfield agreed but was curious why.

"If you cut out that one hour per day and you multiply that by 365 days in a year, that's 365 hours. Divide that by a 40-hour work week and you now have nine and a half weeks of productive time," said Stone. Then he declared, "I want that time."

"What do you want me to do?" asked Canfield.

"I want you to read! Read in your field. Read stories. Read psychology. Read management. Read about marketing. Read about this arena that we play the game in," said Stone. "If you do this, you will not only become more valuable to me but to yourself."[41]

Jack Canfield took Mr. Stone's life-changing advice to heart by establishing a routine of reading a simple dose every day. Consequently, Jack Canfield has gone down in the *Guinness Book of World Records* for writing and selling the most number one bestselling books at the same time from his classic *Chicken Soup for the Soul* series.

What if he'd continued to watch that extra hour of TV each night? We would never know who Jack Canfield is and neither would millions of people where his books have been translated in 80 languages around the world.

MY DAILY ROUTINE

Nicole Crank
Lead Pastor of Faith Church
Daily 5:

1. I spend 15 minutes doing cardio. If I get to do more than that, or if I get to do a workout with weights, I consider it a bonus.

2. I drink a big glass of water with magnesium powder and lemon juice along with a handful of morning vitamins.

3. I do a shot of açai berry juice with cod liver oil, coconut oil and sprinkle in some essential oils.

4. I prepare the same thing for each person of my family and leave it in the refrigerator waiting for them.

5. While I'm drinking tea, I sit down with a daily devotional, my Bible, or a book. I try not to put a time on that space and if I get five quality minutes, that's what I get that day. But sometimes I can get two hours.

Walgreens or Wall Street?

Back when none of us had access to cameras on our phones and we had to take our film to be developed at the photo lab, I would routinely drop off my roll of film at my local Walgreens store. I was there so often that as soon as I entered the sliding doors, I would hear, "Welcome back, Mrs. Foy," by the photo lab technician.

Those were the days when your family vacations and first day of school photos were viewed by a complete stranger before you ever approved them. One day, I ran in the store to pick up another batch of printed memories when the technician said, "I noticed you went to Scotland."

No privacy back then meant he saw all my awkward poses before there was a delete option. I said, "Yes. It's gorgeous. Have you been?"

"No! Are you kidding? But that is the one place in the world I would want to go," he replied.

"So, when are you planning to go?" I asked.

"Never. I could never afford that," he said without hesitation or even a glimmer of possibility.

"What? You can do anything you set your mind to," the motivator in me replied.

"No. I'm not that lucky. But my ancestors are Scottish and I would give anything to go there like you did."

As you can imagine, I had a captive audience to teach the art of goal-setting. This is my specialty. This is my field of study that I've dedicated to learning for years. I was ready to fire away with the inspiration.

"Listen, don't assume it could never happen. Get a piece of paper and write down your dream of going to Scotland. Do the research. Find out how much it costs. How much are the flights? Where can you stay that's most affordable? What if a friend goes with you and you split the hotel cost? Start saving a portion of each paycheck. Look for opportunities to make extra money: mow lawns, have a garage sale, pick up another job. You can do this!" I was cheering him on.

"Noooo....Not me. Like I said, I'm just not that lucky," he replied.

Unfortunately, all my encouragement fell on deaf ears. He refused to dream. He belittled his own possibilities for success. He chose to never go beyond where he was at that moment.

Recently, I was visiting my parents in their hometown where that Walgreens is located, and I ran inside to get some water. Up from the counter popped the same Scottish-blooded young man. "Mrs. Foy, where have you been?"

I wanted to say, "All over the world." But I said, "Hey, I've missed seeing you." Then I explained, "I moved to Rockwall, Texas a few years ago. How have you been?"

He replied, "Just surviving."

"Have you made it to Scotland, yet?" I asked, already knowing the answer.

"No. That would be nice, but I'm not that lucky," he said (again) as he sealed his fate with his own words. He was simply existing another year with no vision. Here he was, an American guy in his late twenties with opportunities all around him and he remained bound to the same place doing the same thing year after year with no hope to ever change.

This young man at Walgreens is similar to another young man from a family devastated from the Great Depression in 1929, who started selling soda and gum from his grandfather's grocery store. A few decades later, he's raking in $20 billion in profit.

What did this young man, Warren Buffet, do that my Walgreens friend won't do? He read books. He opened his mind to possibilities. He expanded his imagination. He gained knowledge. He built his confidence. He gave himself permission to dream outside the four walls of that grocery store.

I'll say it again, successful people don't just read, they read a lot! Why do they read so much? Warren Buffet answered that question when he pointed to a stack of nearby library books and said, "Read 500 pages like this every day. That's how knowledge works. It builds up, like compound interest. All of you can do it, but I guarantee not many of you will do it."[42] Knowledge compounds.

In fact, Mr. Buffet, the most successful financial investor of the 20th century, explains how reading changed the trajectory of his life from grocery store clerk to billionaire investor. "I've had some lucky days in my life," said Buffet, "but the luckiest day was in 1949 when I was 19 years old in Lincoln, Nebraska, and I picked up a copy of *The Intelligent Investor.* It not only changed my investment philosophy; it really changed my whole life." Buffet concludes, "I would be a different person in a different place if I hadn't first seen that book."

Think about those words. He'd be a different person in a different place if he hadn't first picked up that book. The so-called "luck" that my Walgreens friend is hoping for is available to him every day by picking up one book and starting with one page.

What about you? The fact that you're reading right now proves that you're on the right path to change your life. Just don't let this be the only book you read this year! Set goals for yourself to read, whether it's 20 minutes per day or 10 pages a day, a book per month or a book a week. Make it a priority, and you will become a different person in a different place.

Don't Be Average

When the Lord spoke to me in prayer and said, "Don't be average, and your life won't be average," that phrase cautioned me to recognize what the "average" are doing, then do the opposite. If the average person watches four to six hours of TV each day, then don't do that. Cut out even 20 minutes of TV time and go somewhere by yourself to read. If the average college student reads only one book after graduation, then purposefully read as many books as you can get your hands on.

When Jim Rohn was struggling as a 26-year-old American man working a labor job, he met a wealthy gentleman named Earl Shoaf who began to mentor him. Mr. Shoaf was tactful but honest when he reportedly said, "Jim, what you have at this moment in your life, you have attracted by the person you've become!" Shoaf went on to point out, "If you don't have much, perhaps you haven't become much."

Deeply offended by such a bold claim, Rohn held up his paycheck in front of this wealthy man and defended himself by saying, "You don't understand. This is all they pay!"

Shoaf responded, "No. This is all they pay you!" Ouch! Shoaf went on to ask, "Don't they pay others in your company five times this amount?"

"Yes."

His mentor asked, "If you were to qualify for five times this amount, wouldn't your paycheck be five times more?" Shoaf instructed him with this life-changing philosophy that would wind up catapulting Rohn into a worldwide success, "If you develop better skills, you'll earn better income! The key is to become more valuable by changing you!" Shoaf went on to explain, "Don't wish it was easier; wish you were better. Don't wish for less problems; wish for more skills."

I believe this phrase from Earl Shoaf to Jim Rohn has the capacity to change the trajectory of your life (if you let it). Shoaf said, "Learn to work harder on yourself than you do on your job. If you work hard on your job, you'll make a living. If you work hard on yourself, you can make a fortune!"[43] And that's exactly what Rohn did. And so can you!

The Bible says, "To whom much is given, from him much will be required" (Luke 12:48, NKJV). You could rephrase that by saying, "Much will be required in order for much to be given." In other words, to have more, you must become more.

When I teach this concept at conferences, I typically hold up a giant (fake) $100 bill and quote Jim Rohn, "Your money will only grow to the extent that you grow. If you don't like the size of your money—

increase the size of you!"

You could apply that phrase to anything in life.

- Your career will only grow to the extent that you grow.
- Your ministry will only grow to the extent that you grow.
- Your opportunities will only grow to the extent that you grow.
- Your relationships will only grow to the extent that you grow.
- Your vacations will only grow to the extent that you grow.

In fact, any time someone told Rohn they wanted to be a success, he responded, "Take me to your house and show me your library."

He understood that successful people never stop acquiring knowledge in the field related to their purpose. You must have an endless thirst for knowledge if you want to rise above mediocrity and average.

Notice the proof that reading is an essential element for success by checking out how some of the world's most successful people start their day:

- Warren Buffet reads 600-1,000 pages per day.
- Bill Gates reads 50 books each year.
- Mark Cuban reads more than three hours each day.
- Elon Musk would read at least four hours a day growing up.
- Mark Zuckerberg reads one book every two weeks.[44]
- J.K Rowling, the first ever billionaire author, read anything she could get her hands on as a child.

Ask yourself: What did you do last year to grow? How many books did you read? How many hours of TV do you think you watch each day? If you were to cut out one hour, do you think it would benefit you? I hope I've convinced you it would...dramatically. This is how you move forward each day by 1% with a simple 20-minute dose of reading.

Michael Jordan's coach, Tim Grover said, "The body has limitations, the mind does not."[45]

> **"It is what you read when you don't
> have to that determines what you will
> be when you can't help it."**
> - Oscar Wilde

The Reading Habits of Successful People

1. They are intentional about reading.

You are what you read. That's why successful people schedule time for it. They aren't haphazard about investing in themselves; they are intentional. From dusk till dawn, the lives of high achievers are planned out. They are strategic in mapping out how they spend their time each day, and reading is a top priority.

Let me warn you, in the beginning, to not *overachieve* with this habit. If you are not an avid reader, and perhaps like me, you vowed to never study again, start small. Don't start with a goal of reading a book per week.

Make an appointment with yourself to start with a 20-minute plan each day. And stick to it. Do not neglect this commitment. After thirty days of persistence, you will have learned 10 hours' worth of wisdom that could provide you with the idea you need to double your business, to make a major career change, to get your body in shape, to see healing in your marriage, or to get your financial situation straightened out. All in a short 20-minute appointment with yourself each day!

Tony Robbins credits much of his success to his morning ritual which he coined "The Hour of Power." In that hour, he includes 20 minutes of reading every day. Motivational legend, Brian Tracy reads every day and in turn has the knowledge in his field to write an average of four books per year and run three businesses.

74

John Maxwell said, "The greatest influence on my life came from books. They have formed me into who I am today. How I think, and what I feel, have all been formed by what I read."

When you start a daily routine of reading for 20 minutes, initially it may feel like a useless, meaningless, waste of time. It may seem like others are so far ahead of you! You might even think, "Why bother?"

That's exactly how I felt when I began opening chapter one, page one, while setting the alarm on my phone for 20 minutes; but I did it again the next day and the next day. Sixteen years later, I'm surrounded by a library full of wisdom that's compounded from a simple dose of 20 minutes per day.

2. They are selective about what they read.

> **"The more that you read, the more things you will know. The more that you learn, the more places you'll go."**
> **- Dr. Seuss**

Being an avid reader does not ensure your success; however, successful people are avid readers. To the successful, reading is not a simple act of staring at words on a page. They understand the profound effect that consuming a text can have on the mind, and how books can change a person's life.

In his research, Tom Corley discovered that some lower income people do read, but 79% read for entertainment (gossip magazines and celebrity sightings). On the contrary, 94% of wealthy people read to continually improve their own lives.[46] Your mindset is affected by what you consistently put in your mind.

A book is literally the advice, the experience, and the wisdom of a person you admire sitting down and sharing everything they know with you.

If you want to become a bodybuilder, Arnold Schwarzenegger has provided the equivalent of years of personal training in his classic book, *The New Encyclopedia of Modern Bodybuilding*. Why would you need to have a 30-minute phone conversation with the man who wrote 800 pages of answers to all your questions?

If you are determined to get out of debt, Dave Ramsey gave you a step-by-step formula in his bestselling book, *The Total Money Makeover*. He shared his personal story of filing bankruptcy to now experiencing financial peace and prosperity. His personal struggles with money gives you the shortcut to getting out of financial ruin and learning to save, invest, and budget wisely. What took him 20 years to learn, you can apply in one month by reading.

If you desire to be a better leader, start a company, or pastor a church, John Maxwell has over 50 books of the greatest wisdom ever given on leadership. You don't have to try to figure it out on your own. You can learn to build teams, set goals, cast vision, and grow your company all in a simple dose of reading every day.

You can get organized with Julie Morgenstern, learn how to invest with Warren Buffet, improve your thinking with Napoleon Hill, learn to play guitar with Keith Urban, become the most creative home entertainer with Martha Stewart, shorten the time on your breaststroke with Michael Phelps, tell better jokes with Jerry Seinfeld, and apply your eye-liner with precision with Bobbi Brown!

Whichever area you want to improve the most, the experts in their field have laboriously poured their life study into the pages of books all for you. Whether it's pregnancy, parenting, weight loss, retirement planning, or spiritual growth, you have access to everything you need to go to the next level. Find your mentor inside the pages of books.

3. They read to grow.

> **"Write to be understood, speak to be**
> **heard, read to grow."**
> **- Lawrence Clark Powell**

Rather than get paid for doing typical chores such as taking out the trash, making the bed or loading the dishwasher, John Maxwell's father would pay his children to read for 30 minutes each day. Why would he pay them to take out the garbage unless he wanted his children to be garbage men? He told his kids that household chores were just part of being a family, but reading would take them anywhere they wanted to go. He said he put his money where his values were.

Maxwell said that by the time he, his brother, and his sister graduated high school, they were so far ahead of their peers simply because they were assigned to read great books by their father.[47] By the time John Maxwell's brother graduated from college, he was a millionaire. By the time John was 28, he had the tenth largest non-profit organization in the country; by the time his sister was 27, she was running a hospital in Dayton, Ohio. Point well taken.

Where you are is not where you're supposed to stay. God has so much more for your life, but you'll stay small if you keep a small mindset.

There is a story about a man who was out fishing one day when he noticed a peculiar fisherman across the bank. Each time this strange man would catch a big fish, he would toss it back into the water. When he caught a small fish, he would keep it. After watching this unusual practice and seeing his collection of tiny fish grow by the dozens, the observer approached the man and asked, "Why do you throw back all the big fish and keep the small fish?" The fisherman replied, "All I have is a 10-inch frying pan." The moral of this funny story is that this fisherman missed out on something bigger and greater for *his* life because of his limitations.

Brian Tracy said, "You are locked in place at your current level of knowledge and skill. You can go no further with what you now know. Your future largely depends on what you learn and practice from this moment forward."[48]

What could you be missing out on simply because you haven't been exposed to more? Before we see increase on the outside, we must see increase on the inside. Simply put, you can't grow in an area where you have not been exposed. Apostle Paul prayed that "the eyes of your understanding be enlightened" (Ephesians 1:18, NKJV). How do you expose yourself to more? How do you enlighten yourself to more understanding? By reading books.

4. They read to save time and money.

> **"A reader lives a thousand lives before he dies. The man who never reads lives only one."**
> **- George R. R. Martin**

The cheapest way to learn is from others' mistakes. There's a reason why the most successful people look to others for guidance and inspiration through the pages of a book. Learning from others' successes as well as failures enables them to avoid pitfalls and traps that could derail their success. Why wouldn't you learn the art of closing a deal from someone who learned the hard way by losing millions of dollars when it only costs you the price of a $20 book?

Instead of diving head-first into your new venture and relying on your instinct and personal motivation, reading others' experiences gives you a map to bypass the common mistakes of others.

"Our capacity for success and greatness is embodied by the people we surround ourselves with," says author and speaker Lewis Howes. "If we can't hang out with Franklin and Einstein and Tesla, why not surround ourselves with their stories?"[49]

You can save thousands and even millions of dollars by learning from those you admire. They've already been to court, paid the lawsuit, hired the attorney, had sleepless nights, and paid a hefty price to prevent you from going through the same heartache.

Savvy advisers can help you with every phase of your business by sharing their personal roadblocks and costly mistakes to keep you on track. Think of the money you save by reading about the differences in renting or owning a personal vehicle, the upside and downside of purchasing air time for your TV broadcast or radio show, the pros and cons of self-publishing your manuscript or using a book publisher, and the best times of the year to have a fundraiser. Think about it, rather than go into debt after you host your first seminar, you can learn how to gain sponsors who pay for it before it even starts. There's so much wisdom inside those little 5"x 8" paperback books.

It's amazing to think that by dedicating a few minutes each day to reading in a particular field, you could literally become an expert within five years.

5. They seize every moment to learn.

"The book you don't read won't help."
- Jim Rohn

Over 200 successful people, including 7 billionaires, 13 Olympians, and a list of accomplished entrepreneurs were interviewed and asked a simple open-ended question: "What is your number one secret to productivity?" The most common answer? They focus on minutes; not hours.[50] Rather than do what many of us do, allocate our time to one hour or half-hour blocks, successful people utilize the value of every single minute.

"Highly successful people know that there are 1,440 minutes in every day," said Travis Bradbury, "and that there is nothing more valuable than time. Money can be lost and made again, but time spent can never be reclaimed." Olympic gymnast Shannon Miller said, "To this day, I keep a schedule that is almost minute-by-minute."[51] Master your minutes, and you'll master your life.

Successful people may only have 20 minutes before they have to be somewhere, but instead of seeing it as "only 20 minutes," they see it as a 20-minute opportunity that can be spent reading or learning something. They view time as incredibly limited and extremely valuable. They seize every available moment as time to learn something new or accomplish a goal.

Five wasted minutes every day over the course of a year is more than an entire 24 hours (one full day) wasted that could have been spent learning from a good book. Take a small book with you as you commute by bus or train. Download one on your e-reader or smart phone. Carry one in your purse or briefcase as you wait at the doctor's office, wait to board a flight, travel by plane, take your lunch break, sit in the pick up line after school, or lay by the pool. Look for opportunities to read even if it's two pages; it all adds up.

You can learn about retirement investments over breakfast, learn a foreign language over lunch, and learn how to win friends and influence people over dinner. Don't wait for the one hour you don't have; start with the five minutes you do have and open up to chapter one. Seize every available moment to grow yourself, to learn something new and to expand your thinking. Dedicating 15-20 minutes each morning will enable you to be more productive the rest of the day and fill your mind with new ideas and patterns of thinking.

As my pastor, Keith Craft says, "When you elevate your thinking, you'll elevate your life."

6. They read to be inspired.

"The man who does not read good books has no advantage over the man who can't read."
- Mark Twain

As I am writing this portion of the book, I have just concluded a conference near Amsterdam in the Netherlands. I am only two blocks away from the famous house of Anne Frank, author of *The Diary of a Young Girl*. Learning how this teenage girl was given a diary by her father for her thirteenth birthday and how it kept her going as she hid for two years during the Nazi occupation of the Netherlands can adjust the way you think about your personal circumstances. Reading how a young girl stayed motivated to get up each day and cope in such a fear-filled experience for over 24 months can alter your perception of the hardships you're going through and gain a better outlook on where you're headed.

Successful people, however, read biographies and memoirs to gain the grit they see in those they admire. Author and philosopher, James Allen said, "People are anxious to improve their circumstances, but they are unwilling to improve themselves. They therefore remain bound."

Reading inspires us with stories of courage, bravery, and endurance. Reading allows us to see outside of our own challenges and imagine life from another angle. It causes us to avoid self-pity, gain perspective, and be motivated to forge ahead with determination.

Imagine fueling yourself with a shot of inspiration every single morning. I guarantee you would not remain where you are today by this time next year. You would gain ambition you've never had before, eliminate excuses that stopped you in the past, and overcome obstacles that use to appear insurmountable. All because of the inspiration gleaned from reading others' stories. Books are your most profitable investment no matter what field or career you pursue.

7. They apply what they read.

**"To read without reflecting is like
eating without digesting."
- Edmund Burke**

High-achievers rise to the top because they have spent their time learning. When they pick up a book, they don't read it just to finish it but to take something away from it. They apply the knowledge they've gained immediately.

When I was working a full-time job as a media director as well as a part-time job as a youth pastor, (while raising a four-year-old little girl who had ballet and dance lessons), I was so stressed out trying to figure out how to manage everything as well as grocery shop, pay bills, do laundry, prepare messages, host youth events at my house, train youth leaders, and be a good wife, stay fit, and keep the house clean. I had no idea how to handle it all.

Out of pure desperation, I bought a book called *Time Management from the Inside Out* by Julie Morgenstern. That was in the early days of my investment in reading. It was major progress that I even went in a bookstore and spent money on education; however, it sat on my nightstand for months because I could never *find time* to learn how to manage my time! Finally, I seized every pocket of time I could find to read one paragraph even for five minutes. I began to learn practical but life-changing wisdom. For example, I learned to designate certain days to certain tasks. Do laundry on Saturday mornings, pay bills Sunday evening, exercise each morning at 7:00 a.m., grocery shop Monday evenings, etc.

When I began assigning days to my chores, I wasn't stressed out on Thursday morning when I glanced over at the pile of dirty towels across the bathtub. I placed them in the laundry basket and didn't think about laundry again until Saturday morning, laundry day. I was no longer on edge when I collected my mail Tuesday evening after work and saw the pile of bills accumulating. Why? Because I paid bills Sunday evening so I didn't think about them on Tuesday. In the bill box they went, and I moved on.

That simple bit of advice that started with laundry and bills led to blocking out time to write books, prepare TV broadcasts, and record podcasts viewed by millions across the globe.

Successful people are continually on a quest to learn, to grow, to obtain knowledge, and skills that move their lives to new heights. Research even proved that reading is the best way to reduce stress. The more wisdom and knowledge you gain, the more equipped you are to handle any challenge you face.

Reading is to the mind what exercise is to the body. Great readers see the brain as a muscle that needs to be worked. Like going to the gym every day to keep your body fit, reading keeps your mind sharp. Successful people never stop exercising their mind.

MY DAILY ROUTINE

David Crank
Lead Pastor of Faith Church
Daily 5:

1. The first thing I do every morning when my brain is sluggish is listen to my spirit. And then of course I get in the Word and pray for a little bit.

2. After I listen to my spirit, I write in my prayer journal. Because I believe the shortest pencil is greater than the longest memory. I journal every single day because I can look back and notice how history repeats itself and avoid obstacles that are reoccurring.

3. I work out.

4. I listen to a podcast on double speed while I work out.

5. I drink a green smoothie and take my first set of vitamins.

5

RETRAIN YOUR MIND

HABIT #3: LISTEN TO AUDIOS

❝❝I have spent time with Michael Jordan, Bill Gates, TD Jakes, Joyce Meyer, Tony Robbins and Steve Jobs," my friend nonchalantly announced while speaking at a leadership conference. My jaw dropped open in astonishment at the network he had attained and the amount of influence he had developed to be able to connect with these super successful people. That is, until his next statement was: "...But I've never met any of them." *What?* I thought, *I'm confused.*

He said, "I *spend time* with them every morning on my way to work and every evening on my way home as I listen to their audios." This friend is now the pastor of one of the largest churches in America. That's when I realized that the most successful people in the world go to "Automobile University." They use their drive time to listen to motivational teaching. They grow as they go...everywhere.

Whether it's for five minutes while dropping off the dry cleaning or the 45-minute commute to the office, it could be waiting in line to pick up their kids at school, or waiting for a train to pass, they utilize every opportunity to grow, learn, and improve their mindset for success. In fact, Tom Corley discovered in his book, *Rich Habits*, that 63% of wealthy people listen to audiobooks during their commute to work versus 5% of the poor.

This is, by far, the easiest habit to adopt into your current routine to drastically change your thinking and retrain your mind. It requires little effort on your part, but the results are some of the most rewarding of anything you will ever do in your life. I refer to this habit in two little words: Push Play.

When I began this disciplined life in 2002, this habit involved locating an audio device (back then it was a large CD player or boombox) and getting my hands on some encouraging audio messages that I could listen to consistently. My mind was filled with negativity, debilitating thoughts, and fearful images of where my life was headed. The antidote to such a destructive mindset is found in God's Word: "Be transformed by the renewing of your mind" (Romans 12:2, NIV). In other words, we must renew our minds if we want to transform our lives. No doubt, I wanted transformation.

Your thinking has to change for your life to change. Everything gets its start in the mind. So how do you renew your mind? The number one method God has given us to start this practice is found in Romans 10:17. "Faith comes by hearing and hearing by the Word of God." Aka: Push play. Also notice the verse says, "hearing and hearing." In other words, it's a continual practice.

As I mentioned in Chapter 2, I was not disciplined when I started out, so I needed all the help I could get and all the reminders I could find to keep me on track. I grabbed a hot pink Post-it note and scribbled in bold letters: Push play. I stuck it on my bathroom mirror so I couldn't miss it the next morning as I grabbed my toothbrush.

"Oh yeah...push play!" That first morning, the routine began. And the next, and the next until I was able to remove the tacky reminder and simply connect brushing teeth with pushing a button. The more I listened, the more my mind would stop thinking about how messed up my life had become. The more I heard, the more I learned. The more I learned, the more I wanted to learn. My bathroom ritual of listening

to messages inspired me to seize every opportunity I could find to hear more. I was literally getting smarter every time I drove my little girl to school, loaded the dishwasher, folded the laundry, made the beds, deposited my paycheck at the bank, and went to and from work while everybody else was singing their favorite songs.

My mind has been renewed and my life has improved in phenomenal ways due to this elementary habit that requires the least amount of discipline than any of them. You don't have to allocate time on your schedule. You don't have to stop what you're doing. You don't even have to force yourself to exert more energy than you're currently expending. You just use your pointer finger and press the little arrow-shaped button until you hear something audible! It's mind-boggling what those two steps can produce in your life.

Notice the scripture says what we can expect when we push play: "*Faith comes* by hearing and hearing by the Word of God." Every time you hear God's Word, your faith grows. Faith is what you desperately need to live your dreams. Faith is the medicine required to overcome your fears. See, faith and fear are two completely opposite forces trying to work in your life. You can't be full of both at the same time. You're either full of fear or full of faith; it all depends on what you feed the most.

Fear is the number one killer of dreams. We fear rejection, embarrassment, messing up, losing, failing, and making a fool of ourselves. Throughout life there are only two kinds of people: Those who let fear run their lives and those who let faith lead them to their dreams. The best way to defeat fear and get built up on faith is to listen to faith more than you listen to fear. So, if your fears are stopping you from your dreams, push play.

Get Motivated in 30 Seconds

I'll never forget one morning in 2004 when I woke up discouraged. For whatever reason, my mind was focused more on the bad memories of my past than my dreams for the future. I went through my daily five, drove to work, and walked into my office still not fully encouraged. As I was sitting at my desk going through the motions, my co-worker walked in and asked if I wanted to view the new opening segment for the TV broadcast we were launching. Since I was over the Media Department, it was part of my job to approve or disapprove programming changes.

As I walked into the editing room, he pushed play, and this is what I heard shouting across the screen and through the speakers:

"Don't you ever say again that you can't take any more! You can take anything the enemy dishes out! You're a child of the Most High God! You're not a victim; you're a victor! The blood of Jesus flows through your veins. You're a champion, hallelujah!"

In less than 30 seconds, my mindset changed. After listening to that powerful, high energy video clip of my dad preaching, I left the editing room with a completely different outlook on life. I was able to get control over my mood, my emotions, my negative thinking, and shift my thoughts in a positive direction...in less than one minute! That's the power of listening and retraining your mind by hearing God's Word.

What could happen if you scheduled at least one minute of motivation in your routine? I'm convinced you won't accept depression, you won't entertain anxiety, and you won't settle for mediocrity. Your mindset will be elevated as a result of what your ears are hearing.

Success in any area of life is based on a mindset. You will win or lose in life based on what's going on in your thought life, and your thinking is a result of what you're listening to. Whoever has your ear has your life. Whatever is going on in your mind is what you're in the process of manifesting, good or bad. Philosopher James Allen said, "You are today where your thoughts have brought you; you will be tomorrow where your thoughts take you."[52]

In other words, you will produce in your life the dominating *thoughts* in your mind. Joyce Meyer says it this way, "Where the mind goes, the man follows." So, isn't it vitally important that you feed your mind with thoughts that lead you in the direction you want your life to go? Absolutely. And it's not difficult.

This habit of pushing play each morning has not only given me a strong foundation in God's Word but it's led to my learning time management, leadership, financial planning, fitness tips, and even refreshed my French speaking skills. You can learn anything you want to learn and drastically change the direction of your life by listening. What you feed your mind becomes the fruit of your life.

How Powerful are Your Thoughts?

In a well-known study involving 180 patients with knee pain, doctors randomly separated them into three groups. One group received surgery to cut away and remove loose cartilage. The second underwent arthroscopic lavage (in which bad cartilage was flushed out). And the third group were given the signs of surgery but no actual treatment. The patients in the third group who underwent the pretend surgery received anesthesia and incisions on the knee, as if to insert surgical instruments. The remarkable thing is that two years later, without any knowledge of the actual procedure done to them, patients who received no treatment whatsoever reported the same amount of relief as those who received actual treatments. Doctors concluded from their experiment that the mind believed and expected it would be healed, so it was.[53]

Your thoughts are powerful. If you're always thinking that you'll never have any money, you'll always come up short. If you're continually thinking you'll never be promoted, you'll remain under paid. If you're consistently thinking you'll never be this disciplined, you'll continue to struggle with good habits. You will win or lose based on what is going on in your mind! So the goal is to renew our minds for success by intentionally feeding it successful thoughts.

MY DAILY ROUTINE

Stewart Scothorn
CEO of The Benefit Link
Daily 5:

1. The first thing I do when my feet hit the floor is to say aloud three times, "Praise God!" I have no formula or reason, it just works for me.

2. I spend the next hour meditating on God's Word and spending quiet time with the Lord. Then I pray with my wife over our day.

3. I work out for one hour and listen to Christian music. This helps me care for the temple God has given me and builds my spirit at the same time.

4. For breakfast I drink a protein shake with many fruits and vegetables.

5. While I get ready, I listen to a message from one of my favorite preachers.

How to Retrain Your Mind by Listening

This habit of listening to faith-building audios is an important key to success. But here, I want to give you a few more thoughts on how you can retrain and renew your mind. Remember the scripture tells us that faith comes by hearing. Well, that happens in so many ways. Here are some ways that I want you to listen, not only through audios but also as you speak out affirming words and express your gratitude. Let me show you how to pay attention to what and who you are listening to.

1. Invest in yourself.

Investing in yourself has the best returns on investments you can ever make. Warren Buffet said that when he was a young man, he couldn't even talk in front of people. He was so nervous, insecure, and felt inadequate. He withdrew $100 from his account and invested in a Dale Carnegie course for personal development, and it absolutely changed his life. Buffet said, "The best investment you'll ever make is in yourself. It pays 1000 to 1."[54]

Think about it. If you took everything away from Richard Branson—the wealthiest man in the U.K., worth $5 billion, who runs 400 companies—and threw him out on the street with nothing but the clothes on his back, he would be right back in a penthouse apartment living his lavish lifestyle in no time. Why? How? What does he have that others don't have?

Human capital.

He has wisdom, knowledge, competency, skills, and experience that led him to the success he has attained. And nobody can take that away. Human capital is a real thing, and it's defined as "the stock of competencies, knowledge, social and personality attributes, including creativity, embodied in the ability to perform labor so as to produce economic value." Branson could work his way back to a Fortune 500 company based on his human capital and personal investment through the years…and so could you. But you must become more by investing in your most valuable asset: you.

I will never forget the first time I put my own money on the line to buy new audio teachings and books. After I had practically worn out my parents' audios that I sorta stole from their house, it was time for some new messages. Because I was vividly seeing for myself the positive impact audios were having on my life, I wanted more. I visited a minister's website and went on a shopping spree of wisdom.

It was like a smorgasbord of motivation: "How to build your

confidence," "How to overcome fear and doubt," "The keys to a successful mindset," "Break free from your past," "The power of determination." All I could think was "Add to cart." I was shocked when the total came to $60! "Sixty dollars? I'm not going to spend sixty bucks on faith-building resources! That's ridiculous!" I said to myself. Then, I thought, "I would easily spend this amount on new clothes. This is helping me get a new mindset! My future is worth $60!" And I pushed "Pay."

When that little brown box arrived on the front doorstep, I thought I struck a gold mine. I could hardly wait to run upstairs to my giant boombox, put the CD in and start learning! Today, I can honestly say that the most valuable items in my house are not my Louis Vuitton handbags, the Louboutin shoes, or the stunning diamond ring Rodney bought me for our 25th wedding anniversary. (Sorry, Rod!) My most valuable items are on my shelf in my personal library! Those audios, books, and resources stacked in my home office are what transformed my life from the inside out.

Today, when I sit at a table to discuss marketing ideas, financial investing, spiritual guidance, the benefits of fasting, leading teams in personal growth, or even 21 ways to use a resistance band, I have something valuable to say! I've been asked, "How do you know this stuff?" My answer is through the simple act of pushing play each morning while I add more mascara or drive through Rockwall, Texas on my way to work.

What is a "programmed for greatness" mindset worth to you? We tend to invest in the latest appliances, the daily latte, the mani/pedi, and the dinner outings with friends, but far too often we neglect the greatest use of our finances which is investing in ourselves. When you invest in yourself, a whole new world of opportunities will open up for you. Unlike other investments out there, investing in yourself is never a risk. It always pays off.

2. Seize every opportunity to grow.

In habit #2, I encouraged you to read as many books as possible in your lifetime, that discipline requires dedicated, concentrated time to stop everything and focus your eyes on the pages of a book. However, this habit doesn't demand anything different from your current lifestyle other than replacing what you're currently hearing with something you should be hearing. And the best way to do that is by going to "Automobile University," a phrase coined by the great Zig Ziglar.

Ziglar tells a story about a man named Stephen Payne who struggled most of his life. At 18 years old, he qualified for his GED but was 22 before he earned a high school diploma. Proving that it's never too late to get a grip on greatness, at the age of 43, Payne got serious about his life. He began utilizing every moment behind the wheel of his car and took full advantage of these precious minutes by listening to audios everywhere he traveled.

"He became a full-time student at Automobile University," said Ziglar, "And as a result, he speaks Spanish and French so fluently that he is now translating and interpreting for his company. He also speaks Italian and is in the process of learning both German and Japanese as well as Latin and his own Cherokee language."[55]

You can learn everything from the art of negotiating, and how to prepare winning presentations, to how to raise exceptional children, 51 crockpot meals to prepare, how to earn $3,000 decluttering your house, or how to start a company from scratch...all before you even get to the grocery store.

One Christmas season, I was out running holiday shopping errands while listening to Dave Ramsey's audiobook, *The Total Money Makeover*. In less time than it took to get from my house to the mall, I gathered the information I needed to completely pay off my car! That one simple decision to push play during my commute to go Christmas shopping enabled me to save thousands of dollars in interest payments over the next three years.

You have access to an entire library of audios at your fingertips. Podcasts are available on tons of apps. Audiobooks and MP3s are easy to download on your smart phones and tablets. You don't have to haul a big boombox around like I did to access incredible advice while you commute, drop off the kids, go to the bank, run errands, drive through the car wash, and sit at a red light. This is more valuable than jamming out to your favorite tunes day after day and year after year with no improvement in your life.

One study reported that the average person commutes 30 minutes to and from work each day. Over a five-year period, that's 1,250 hours behind the wheel of your car or the equivalent of a college education. Can you believe that? With "Automobile University," you could earn the equivalent of a university degree during your regular commute to the office.

ABC News published an article with startling statistics of how many hours Americans spend stuck in traffic jams each year—on average 42 hours. That's not including commute time...that's just at a standstill on the road.[56] But your traffic time doesn't have to be wasted. It's all in how you use it.

The Bible says, "Study to show yourself approved" (2 Timothy 2:15, KJV). You can no longer justify your excuse for not learning by saying you don't have time. Grow as you go. UCLA basketball coach, John Wooden said, "When I am through learning, then am I through."[57]

Success is the result of a few small disciplines practiced daily. This is one small discipline will accelerate your results in a big way.

3. Focus your listening.

In the beginning of my quest for knowledge, I was still consumed with the images of my painful past. I couldn't get my hands on enough messages that dealt with forgiveness, self-esteem, freedom from guilt, and overcoming insecurities. I listened to the same messages over and over again until they sunk in. I began applying what I was learning. I discovered how to stop mentally rehashing all the regretful choices I had made. I learned how to hold my head up, pull my shoulders back, and walk with dignity and purpose.

After that season of transformation, I no longer needed the daily dose of emotional freedom, so I moved on to financial wisdom. I consumed my drive time with knowledge from those who had proven keys to paying off debts, building emergency savings accounts, and starting an investment portfolio. As I would learn, I would make a checklist of things I wasn't doing but planned to do. Then, I would go down the checklist one by one until I accomplished each goal.

Whatever you're struggling with or feeling most compelled to study, that's where you need to focus your resources and attention to learning. Become a serious student in that area. Someone said, "It's better to be world class at a *few* things than mediocre at *most* things." More knowledge and information will give you an advantage on the road to success.

Successful people are never satisfied with being average. They realize that average is as close to the bottom as it is the top. Grant Cardone says, "When you get focused on your dream, don't just drink the Kool-Aid. Swim in it."[58] In other words, pour yourself into your dreams and become the best in your field.

One message isn't enough. It's like taking medicine for a headache. You can't physically see what that pill is doing, but little by little, you experience the effects of it. It's the same with daily doses of wisdom.

I highly encourage you to find a mentor. It may not necessarily be someone you can sit down and have a cupcake with and ask questions. However, you can be mentored through the pages of their books, the sound of their audiobooks, and the wisdom on their podcast.

In fact, the most successful people attribute their success to having mentors. Mark Zuckerberg had Steve Jobs. Bill Gates has Warren Buffet. Oprah has Barbara Walters. Justin Bieber has Usher. Yves Saint Laurent had Christian Dior. Quincy Jones had Ray Charles. Lady Gaga has Elton John. Terri Savelle Foy has Joyce Meyer.

Make a list of everyone you know who has a lot of experience in your area of struggle or your area of interest. If they specialize in writing music, starting businesses, acquiring real estate, etc., get your hands on their products.

Set yourself up for success by researching the resources you need right now. Have it ready to go tomorrow morning so you can *push play* when you head off for your normal commute. Whether it's downloading an audiobook or a podcast or ordering resources online, get it ready to go.

Remember, God *will* change your circumstances, but He'll change you first.

4. Make positive declarations.

**"Be careful how you think; your life is
shaped by your thoughts."
- Proverbs 4:23, GNT**

Dr. Daniel Amen said, "Don't believe everything you hear—even in your own mind."[59] Your thoughts are the pathway to your destiny. We know how powerful our thoughts are in leading and guiding our lives. In fact, your life goes in the direction of what you think about the most—positively or negatively. So, how do you get control over your thought life? How do you shut your negative thoughts down and retrain your mind for success?

The key to getting control of your thought life has to do with what is coming out of *your mouth*. What you repeatedly hear, you eventually believe. And you believe yourself more than anyone else. Your mouth is the most powerful tool you have. It is the weapon in combating your own worst thoughts.

Every thought you think and every word you speak is an affirmation. How do you know what someone is thinking? Listen to what they say. Your mouth indicates what your heart is thinking. You're using affirmations every moment whether you realize it or not. You have to get your mouth lined up with what you believe and what you desire in your life if you want to have positive change.

"Out of the abundance of the heart, the mouth speaks" (Luke 6:45 NKJV). What you listen to and put in your heart will inform what comes out of your mouth. If you are listening to faith-building messages and audios, then faith and dreams will come out of your mouth.

If you want to know where your life is headed, listen to the words coming out of your mouth. We must retrain our thinking by intentionally speaking positive words over our circumstances. When I talk about making positive declarations, I mean consciously choosing words that will either help eliminate negativity from your life or help create something positive in your life.

Let me explain. You can't defeat thoughts with other thoughts. You defeat negative thoughts with words. You can't try so hard to think about something else until your bad thoughts go away. It's only a matter of time before your mind will go right back to where it wanted to be.

But imagine if I asked you to multiply your current age by 75. As you're doing the math in your head, what if I interrupted you and asked you to give me directions to your house. You would have to stop working the math problem to hear what your mouth was saying. Your words, giving me directions, would take over the thoughts about the math problem. Try it.

So, when negative, fearful, or debilitating thoughts are being entertained in your mind, the key to overcoming them is to start speaking positive, faith-filled words, out loud, out of your own mouth.

Yes, I know what you're thinking, "That's crazy!" You might be a little confused if you've never spent time learning the power of words. The Bible says, "David encouraged *himself* in the Lord" (1 Samuel 30:6, KJV). Interview any successful person and they'll tell you how important positive self-talk is to your success.

In an interview with Conor McGregor, the UFC champion was asked, "If someone had told you when you were little that you would have this much success, what would you have said?"

McGregor responded, "I believe you! That's what I would have said because I did believe!" He explained, "I had a small, small group of people telling me that back then. Other than that, it was ME telling myself!"

Whether McGregor knows it or not, he was practicing the Word of God. James 3:4-5 tells us the same way a ship's rudder controls the direction the ship sails, your tongue controls the direction of your life! Your words are prophesying your future.

The psalmist David said, "I will say of the Lord, He is my refuge and my fortress" (Psalm 91:2, KJV). The verses that follow say that God will deliver him, protect him, cover him, etc. Notice the connection: I will *say*, and He will *do*.

It doesn't say, "*I believe* He's my refuge. *I believe* He's my strength." No, the psalmist *spoke* it out! Then God became his refuge and his strength. In other words, if you're bold enough to speak it, God is bold enough to do it. You can't have what you say if you don't say anything! Think of the opposite of this verse: "I will *not* say of the Lord, and He will *not* do." Those are the results you'll get if you do not speak!

The Lord has taught me that it's not enough to stop saying wrong, negative things; I also had to start saying the right, positive thing. While negative words will keep you from being what God wants you to be, positive words will lead you to where God wants you to go.

Proverbs 6:2 says, "You are snared by the words of your mouth"

(NKJV). Your negative talk will trap you in a life you don't want. Start asking yourself, "Is what I'm about to say what I want to come about in my life?" If the answer is no, then don't say it.

As Justin Timberlake said of the critics of your dreams, "Their words will fade; yours won't!"[60]

How you talk to others *and to* yourself will determine how successful you will be. Period. What you say to others isn't nearly as important as what you say to yourself. It's not okay to be critical of yourself. Why? Because you are listening. Your personal self-talk can help you lose weight, get good grades, achieve promotion, close sales, get along with family members, win awards and even gold medals!

Your words are creating the life you are currently living, positively or negatively. James 3:10 says, "Out of the same mouth proceed blessing and cursing" (NKJV). You can curse yourself with your own words or you can bless yourself.

Making positive declarations is something you can start today. Sometimes the smallest changes produce drastic results.

A plastic surgeon was asked what it takes to transform how his clients feel about their appearance. "Two millimeters." He explained, "Lifting someone's nose two millimeters or raising eyelids two millimeters makes all the difference." Most people think it's changing everything, but making a simple two-millimeter change makes the biggest difference.

Changing the way you talk to and about yourself is the two-millimeter difference that will make a drastic change in your mindset. I encourage you today to make a positive "I am" list to start declaring over yourself. Here are a few of my personal declarations from my book *Pep Talk* to get you started.

I declare in the name of Jesus:

I am highly favored of God.
I am proactive.

I am courageous in the pursuit of my dreams.

I am sensitive to God's timing in my life.

I am embracing every opportunity God brings me.

I am always in the right place at the right time.

I am receiving extraordinary opportunities.

I am fulfilling my destiny.

I am open to change.

I am talented and gifted with special qualities.

I am thriving in life.

I am equipped for everything God has for me.

I am rising above every obstacle.

I am preparing for the next level.

I am creative.

I am programmed for success.

I am a person of excellence and integrity.

I am fulfilling my life assignment down to the last detail.

In addition to making positive declarations over yourself and your future, let me add that there is nothing more powerful than speaking God's Word out of your mouth to retrain your mind for success. Declare these scriptures out loud by faith:

- I will be strong and not give up, for my work will be rewarded (2 Chronicles 15:7, NIV).
- God is giving me the desires of my heart and making all my plans succeed (Psalm 20:4, NIV).
- I delight myself in the Lord, and He will give me the desires of my heart (Psalm 37:4-5, NIV).
- I trust in the Lord with all my heart and lean not on my own understanding; in all my ways, I acknowledge Him, and He will direct my path (Proverbs 3:5-6, NKJV).
- I commit to the Lord whatever I do, and He will establish my

plans (Proverbs 16:3, NIV).

- For God has not given me a spirit of fear and timidity, but of power, of love and of self-discipline. (2 Timothy 1:7, NIV).

If you'll change what you're *saying*, you'll change what you're *seeing*!

5. Express Gratitude.

Have you ever met an unhappy person who was grateful or a happy person who was ungrateful? Probably not.

Expressing gratitude is one of the greatest habits to retrain your mind for success. Recognizing what you have to be grateful for forces your mind to extract the negative and focus on the positive. Arianna Huffington, co-founder and editor-in-chief of *The Huffington Post*, wrote, "Gratitude works its magic by serving as an antidote to negative emotions. It's like white blood cells for the soul, protecting us from cynicism, entitlement, anger, and resignation."[61]

Positive thinking leads to a positive outcome. In a *Business Insider* article, Faisal Hoque agrees, "When we consciously practice an attitude of gratitude, things don't just look better—they really do get better."[62] And positive thinking only happens when what you listen to and put in your heart is positive as well.

Successful people are grateful people. This is where we see the Law of Attraction in action. When you're grateful, you attract more to be grateful for. The adverse is true as well. When you complain, you attract more to complain about. How do you change a lousy, self-pity, complaining, discouraged attitude? With appreciation.

> **"Say thank you in advance for what's already yours. That's how I live my life. That's one of the reasons I am where I am today."**
> **- Denzel Washington**

The University of Massachusetts Dartmouth did an in-depth study on the effects of gratitude and discovered how much it contributes to your rate of success. One of their findings states, "Daily discussion of gratitude results in higher reported levels of alertness, enthusiasm, determination, attentiveness, energy, and sleep duration and quality."[63]

Oprah Winfrey, one of the wealthiest women in the world, reminds us, "Be thankful for what you have and you'll end up having more. If you concentrate on what you don't have, you will never, ever have enough." The benefits of expressing gratitude to retrain your mind are endless. Successful entrepreneurs, celebrities, authors, and innovators such as Tim Tebow, Suze Orman, Clint Eastwood, and Steve Harvey consciously practice a lifestyle of expressing gratitude. Founder of John Paul Mitchell, John Paul DeJoria says, "For the most part, I can't tell you how important it is to take those first five minutes [of the day] and be thankful for life."[64]

Two of the most powerful words in the English language are "Thank you." It's one of the most easily recognized phrases in any foreign language regardless of your fluency. Whether it's *merci, gracias, danke,* or *mahalo*, it's universally recommended that you learn this expression before you visit a country abroad. Well, I've discovered that saying thank you isn't just appreciated overseas, it also touches the heart of God and is a vital key to living your dreams.

God makes several references to thanksgiving throughout the Bible:

- "Do not be anxious about anything, but in every situation, by prayer and petition, *with thanksgiving*, present your requests to God. And the peace of God, which transcends all understanding, will guard your hearts and your minds in Christ Jesus" (Philippians 4:6-7, NIV).
- "Enter his gates *with thanksgiving* and his courts with praise; give thanks to him and praise his name" (Psalm 100:4, NIV).
- "Give *thanks* in all circumstances; for this is God's will for you

in Christ Jesus" (1 Thessalonians 5:18, NIV).

- "Be thankful and say so" (Psalm 100:4, AMPC).

Journal Your Gratitude

Your habits will tend to overlap and work together. So as you pray and meditate, you will notice the blessings in your life, and you'll feel grateful. As you read and listen, you will watch yourself and your surrounding grow, and you'll feel grateful. As you see your dream and goals being achieved, you'll be so grateful. As you watch and feel your body become healthier, you'll be grateful. Record it. Just as we talked about journaling in the last habit, I want you to journal the gratitude you experience as these habits begin to change your situation.

One of the greatest ways to shift your thoughts from negative to positive is to start journaling your gratitude. This is a simple exercise that I began practicing years ago in order to magnify the good and truly show God how grateful I am for every single thing He's done. As a result, my pages keep filling up with more and more appreciation. A grateful heart is a magnet for miracles.

Tips to Keeping a Gratitude Journal

1. Write 3-5 things you're grateful for each day. You can do this during your prayer/meditation habit. Make sure you do it at the same time each day to make it habitual. But don't just write it. Say it out loud. Remember you believe yourself more than you believe anyone else. You can talk yourself into a grateful attitude even when you don't feel like it!

2. Listen and write whatever comes up in your heart. It doesn't have to be big things like a raise, a new car, or an exotic vacation. It can be as simple as your day off spent at home, the sun

shining, the cupcake your friend brought you, or the new book you purchased. Magnifying what you already have only leads to attracting more things to be grateful for. Write as big or as small as you want. The point is that you recognize what you have and you truly

appreciate it.

3. Don't complain. Practice giving no attention to the frustrating things around you. Don't shine a light on any negativity. That means don't complain about the weather, the traffic, the line at the grocery store, the way you slept, how hungry you are, your body, or your headache. Nothing. I'll be the first to warn you— it's not easy! But it's an excellent discipline to retrain your mind for success. When a complaint starts to roll off your tongue, catch it! Guard your complaints as if your life depends on it. Why? Because it does. When you complain, you only attract more to complain about.

4. Practice this for 30 days. Journal your gratitude and avoid complaining for 30 days straight. I'm telling you from my experience and from the testimonies of thousands, your life will be on a path to success. God will open doors in your life that you never dreamed possible, because you're acknowledging His ways and giving no attention to the distractions and complaints around you. The more gratitude you express, the more abundance

you experience.

MY DAILY ROUTINE

Diana Scothorn

Founder and Owner of The Benefit Link

Daily 5:

1. Wake up at 4:00 a.m. My husband and I wrap our arms around each other and pray together! We have declarations we repeat daily, in our prayer time. We have been doing this faithfully for almost 10 years now.

2. Before I do anything else I make my bed, proceed to the kitchen and drink 16 ounces of water, take my vitamins, and get my things ready for work.

3. My personal one-on-one time with God is an appointment that I always keep, and it is not up for negotiations! I make time to review personal and work goals, journal and make positive declarations over my life.

4. Hit the gym! While I am on the elliptical I listen to motivational speakers, ministers or praise music.

5. As I get ready, I listen to God's Word, and while I am driving to and from work I listen to Joel Osteen. His upbeat encouragement keeps my focus off me and on what really matters!

6

HOW TO SET & ACHIEVE ANY GOAL YOU HAVE IN LIFE

HABIT #4: WRITE (AND REVIEW) YOUR DREAMS AND GOALS

With pen in hand and a spiral notebook in my lap, I began writing what I thought was a simple to-do list: clean the kitchen, finish reading the book, have a garage sale, raise an extra $1200, pay off the MasterCard bill of $1178, get the car washed, go to New Orleans to see Jodi, etc. The list was important to me because it gave me more reasons to get up and go after something when the rest of my life was in disarray.

Little did I know that this simple habit was the secret of success for over 500 millionaires researched in Napoleon Hill's classic book *Think and Grow Rich*. I didn't know this was the habit Jim Carrey practiced which led to him earning $10 million filming *Dumb and Dumber*. I had no idea Arnold Schwarzenegger modeled this habit as a teenager in Austria with a dream of being a bodybuilder.

At the time, I never would have dreamed this simple habit would lead to bigger to-do lists including: write the book, get a French publisher, see my books in bookstores, obtain offices, launch a TV show, pay off the car, etc. Successful people share this common habit, and it is one you simply must develop: Write and review your dreams and goals.

If there's one habit that I am known for more than any other, it is having a vision, writing it down, and keeping it before my eyes. People stop me in department stores saying, "You're that vision board lady!" The truth is that once I learned the secret to setting goals, getting laser-focused on a vision, and taking action, my life catapulted to new levels I never thought possible.

When I was first writing my to-do lists and random goals, I had no idea how powerful a pen and paper would become in my life. Without even knowing it, I began thinking beyond my present reality and designing my destiny.

I'll never forget sitting in my guest bedroom with my laptop and giving myself permission to dream as big as I could. For the first time, I was thinking beyond getting the laundry done or the living room organized. Even alone with my thoughts, I was embarrassed to admit what I saw in my future. Feelings of inadequacy pressed against me. Who was I to think I had the right to dream this big? But I pushed it all aside and imagined it was the year 2011, five years in my future.

With my eyes closed tight, I imagined what I could accomplish in those five years if I truly believed anything was possible. I listed five enormous impossibilities: (1) Minister on TV, (2) Write a book, (3) Host a women's conference, (4) Start an outreach to young women (with unexpected pregnancies, or rescued from human trafficking, etc.), and (5) Start a mission in France. Each of these crazy dreams were so outside the realm of possibility, but for some reason, once I took the time to get them out of my doubt-filled head and onto paper, my potential began to rise.

It was almost as if I was sitting behind the steering wheel of a car with no destination in mind until that moment on August 16, 2006, when I "programmed my GPS" and allowed my subconscious mind to pinpoint my route to get to my dream destination. Almost instantly, my life began to move in the direction of the words in that spiral notebook.

Within five years, every single "impossible dream" in that notebook was a reality in my life. By August 16, 2011 (five years later), I was co-hosting a weekly television broadcast with my dad, Jerry Savelle. I had already written two books and seen them on the shelves in my local bookstore. I launched a women's conference called "Icing" in 2010 which has grown to thousands of women in attendance. I reached out to girls' homes, safe houses, and shelters for young women giving them my books and resources to help them get a vision for their lives. And I began ministering in the nation of France in 2008 and obtained a French publisher who now translates all my books in French. Here's the kicker: not one single dream (of the five) even took the full five years to accomplish.

What could *you* accomplish if you programmed your GPS today? I am convinced the next five years of your life could be the most amazing, most phenomenal years thus far...or they could be just another five years. It's entirely up to you!

What's On Your Life List?

In her Ted Talk, Kimberly Rich reports a study that surveyed 600 people in their 70's to understand which caused greater regret: the things that we did or the things we never did.

The elderly interviewed were asked, "If you could live your life over again, what would you do differently?" A staggering 54% regretted all the things they missed out on or wished they had done. What they discovered is that the regret we feel from having made bad decisions in the past lasts at most a couple years; but the regret we experience from what we missed out on lasts a lifetime.[65]

More than half of the people you work with, go to church with, hang out with and live next to will come to the end of their lives with feelings of great disappointment for not having lived their dreams. Don't let that be you!

One of my favorite stories is that of a man nicknamed the "Real Indiana Jones," aka John Goddard. As a young boy, John often heard his parents and their friends discuss how much they regret the things they never did, the countries they never saw, and opportunities they never seized. He determined as a teenager that he would not end up with those sentiments.

At only 15 years old, he went to his bedroom while his parents and their friends were having dinner, got out a piece of paper, and began writing all the things he wanted to do in his lifetime. In essence, he wrote the ultimate bucket list back in 1940.

His elaborate list included experiences such as:
1. Visit a movie studio
2. Learn to play polo
3. Read the Bible from cover to cover
4. Write a book
5. Publish an article in National Geographic Magazine
6. Visit birthplace of Grandfather Sorenson in Denmark
7. Dive in a submarine
8. Ride a horse in the Rose Bowl Parade
9. Land on and take off from an aircraft carrier
10. Ride an elephant, camel, ostrich, and bronco
11. Fly in a blimp, balloon, and glider
12. Teach a college course
13. Learn to fence
14. Learn jujitsu
15. Explore depths of the sea
16. Learn to play flute and violin

17. Make a parachute jump
18. Go on a church mission
19. Learn to fly a plane
20. Photograph Niagara Falls
21. Explore Fiji Islands
22. Climb Mount Kilimanjaro
23. Visit the Great Wall of China
24. Visit the Eiffel Tower
25. Learn French, Spanish, and Arabic
26. Travel through the Grand Canyon by foot and by boat
27. Live to see the 21st Century[66]

And that's not all. His "Life List" included a total of 127 things he wanted to do. (For his complete list visit JohnGoddard.Info.) In an interview on *Dateline NBC*, Goddard said, "There's something about the human spirit that when you accept challenge and work on it and have deadlines and capture your potential, it's astounding what you can do." The remarkable thing is that John Goddard passed away in 2013 at the age of 88 years old having accomplished 120 of the 127 things on his list.

Many of us had dreams as kids, but as we grew up, we were told, "Stop dreaming," "Be realistic," "Stop living in a fantasy," or "Get a real job!" But I want you to dream again! Your imagination is a gift God has given you to set the course for where He wants you to go.

Arnold Schwarzenegger said, "You need a very clear vision of where you want to go. You can have the best ship in the world but if the captain doesn't know where to go, that ship will drift around the world and not end up anywhere. And that's exactly the way it is in real life. If you don't have a goal or a vision, you just drift around. You're not going to be happy."[67]

Instead of taking the easy path, living in a comfort zone that doesn't ignite your passion, I want you to live a fulfilling life in the regret-free zone and start dreaming again. Jack Canfield says, "The one sentence that fills the thoughts of people as they prepare to pass on is this: 'If only I'd done the things I really wanted to do, my life would have been so different.'"[68]

- If only I'd invested 10% of my income every month.
- If only I'd taken care of my health.
- If only I'd written that book that was in my heart.
- If only I'd taken a chance and started my own business.

The someday syndrome is a fatal trap! You could be the greatest enemy to your success by not using your imagination and realizing your true dreams. Give yourself permission to succeed. Make a decision to do what God has put in your heart to do. Stop comparing yourself to what anyone in your family has or hasn't done. This is your life. What is God expecting of you? What do you need to accomplish?

Jeremiah 1:5 says, "I have chosen you and have not cast you away. Before I shaped you in the womb, I knew all about you. Before you saw the light of day, I had holy plans for you" (MSG). God has plans for your life; isn't it time you discovered them and live them out?

The Ripple Effect

There was a guy named Ken who weighed more than 475 pounds. His size did not deter him from going after his dream which included his passion of coaching hockey. He became a great coach, leading a junior club to division championships in five out of six seasons. He had a remarkable record. But his bigger dream was to coach in the National Hockey League.

Ken knew just about everything there was to know about the game of hockey. He also knew how to inspire players to consistently give their top performances. His weight, however, was a major factor. He was told that he probably wouldn't be selected for big-league coaching because of his size.

One day at the end of practice, he slipped and fell on the ice. The fall was humiliating, but even more was the embarrassment of not being able to get back on his feet. The players had to physically pull him up and help him back to the bench.

This was a defining moment for Ken!

He made a choice to take charge of his future! Instead of always saying to himself, "Someday, I'm going to get this weight under control," he got focused, single-minded, and determined on his one major goal! With the support of his friend, he got on a fitness program, training every day and eating healthier meals. Using the power of vision and intent focus, he lost an amazing 250 pounds in less than two years!

Ken stayed committed and focused on his major goal of being promoted as a head coach in the NHL. He made an agreement with himself that he would do whatever it took to compete for a coaching position at the professional level. In 1997, Ken Hitchcock's dream came true when he became the head coach in the National Hockey League for the Dallas Stars.

In his first season, he led the team on a winning streak. Two years later, he achieved every coach's dream in the NHL, winning the Stanley Cup, the first ever championship for the Dallas Stars.[69]

What would Ken's life story be if he had still maintained the mindset of *someday*? Someday, I'll start working out. Someday, I'll eat less. Someday, I'll make a commitment. Someday, I'll get serious about my true dreams. If that were still his mindset, his story would have never made it into this book. His single decision to turn someday into today not only changed his life, but his choices affected an entire team, an entire city, and all the people who know his story.

Who needs to read your story for inspiration? Who needs to hear about your turn around in life, your defining moment, your moment of decision? Think about the ripple effect of good choices. Ken's income increased. His lifestyle increased. His opportunities and life experiences increased. And that affected everyone close to him.

My daughter often tells me, "Thank you, Mama, for choosing to go after your dreams." Why? Because my choices opened up a whole new world for her too. At this moment, Kassidi and I are sitting in a stunning Parisian apartment with the windows open and the sun beaming through our view of the Eiffel Tower. I am speaking in the morning at one of the biggest churches in the nation. My books are translated in French and available down the street in the bookstores of Paris. Everything I just wrote began as a thought in my imagination years ago as I sat in my guest bedroom in Burleson, Texas with a number two pencil and a spiral notebook. And it would have stayed there as a pipe dream had I not learned what I'm going to share with you in this chapter that will take you from where you are to where you want to be.

What could happen in your life if you said it's no longer *someday*, it's today! What could happen if you got laser-focused on your vision, began giving yourself permission to dream, trusted God, and just went for it? I'm convinced you would look back five years from now and say, "Look what God has done in my life! I am not who I used to be."

MY DAILY ROUTINE

Larry Winters
Founder and President of Leadership Team Development
Daily 5:

1. Enter the day with praise and thanksgiving. Thank God for present and future blessings.

2. Mentor at least one person on our business team.

3. Listen to a business audio every morning.

4. Listen to a faith audio every evening.

5. Read a chapter in a success book every day.

5 Steps to Live Your Dreams

I want to share with you what every successful person swears by to drastically improve your life. It doesn't matter if your goal is to lose 100 pounds, appear on the cover of a magazine, write a bestselling book, start an orphanage in Africa, win teacher of the year, or have an apartment in Paris. These are the steps to live your dreams.

1. Visualize your future.

You will never leave where you are until you see where you'd rather be. Where can you see this future place? In your imagination. You have to see where you're headed in the future before you start taking steps towards it in your present. Author Bo Bennett said, "Visualization is daydreaming with a purpose."

> **"Visualize this thing that you want. See it, feel it, believe in it. Make your mental blueprint, and begin to build."**
> **- Robert Collier**

ARE YOU NEAR-SIGHTED?

My husband and I both had Lasik eye surgery years ago, and it was the best money we ever spent. When I was in high school, I discovered how poor my eyesight had become. I couldn't read the chalkboard in class unless I sat up front. I could barely see the scoreboard at the football games, so I was the cheerleader doing backflips when the other team scored! My friends would holler my name down the halls at school, but I couldn't recognize who they were, so I waved enthusiastically to everybody. That's probably the reason I won "Miss Crowley High School!" I acted just as excited to see each person since I didn't have a clue who I was waving at.

I kept my poor vision a secret from my parents because I did not want to wear glasses. Glasses were not cool in 1985. Only Ray-Ban sunglasses were in style, not coke bottle glasses. However, my weak eyesight was drawn out of hiding one embarrassing day. I had to take an eye exam during my driver's education class. Hundreds of new drivers were being tested in the school cafeteria, and I stood in line panic-stricken. I knew I would fail.

All of a sudden, I had a brilliant plan that would help me pass with flying colors. I memorized every single letter the girl in front of me said as she cited what she saw in the little machine. "L-M-Z-P-T-W," she said. (It's been over 30 years, so I don't actually remember the letters, but let's pretend!)

"Next," the teacher said.

I looked in the little machine, couldn't see a thing, but confidently recited, "L-M-Z-P-T-W!" And I stood up straight with a big smile.

The teacher's eyebrows went together, and her head turned to the side in complete confusion. "Honey," (I'm from the South, so everyone says that!) "Are you okay?" she asked, puzzled.

"Yes, ma'am," I said with confidence.

"Could you read them again?" she asked.

"L-M-Z-P-T-W!" I said again, enthusiastically.

"Sweetheart, I think you need to get your eyes professionally checked," she said. "You did not get one letter right."

What I didn't realize was that she switched the screens between each person giving a completely different list of letters to read. She probably thought I was nuts and needed more than my eyes professionally checked!

I got a big *F* on that exam and had to go with my mom to see an optometrist for a thorough evaluation. I'll never forget sitting in the chair squinting to see the first, gigantic letter and hesitantly saying, "E?" (with a big question mark). I couldn't see anything!

The doctor instantly gave the diagnosis and said, "Oh, honey, I know what your problem is. You're near-sighted."

I said, "No. I can't see far stuff. I can't even see you!"

He said, "I know. You're near-sighted."

The optometrist explained that being near-sighted means that you can see only what's near you. I like how Pastor Chris Hodges said, "It's the only medical field that names your condition for what you're good at." It's like going to the doctor with a broken arm and the doctor says, "Well, your leg works great!"

Here's the interesting thing. On the way home with my corrective lenses in, I was mesmerized looking out the window as my mom drove. Don't laugh, but I had no idea that most people could see the actual leaves on the trees. I had gotten so accustomed to only seeing a big green blur that I thought it was normal. Now, I could read the white letters of a stop sign rather than see a big red octagon shape on the side of the road. Over time, my eyes had deteriorated, but I didn't even realize it.

I got so used to only seeing what was right in front of me that I lost all sight of anything in the distance. Maybe that's your diagnosis today. You can't see beyond what's directly in front of you. You're near-sighted, and you can't even catch a glimpse of what's in your future.

In fact, you can tell if someone is near-sighted by how they talk. If all you talk about is how bad things are and that they'll never change, you're near-sighted. If all you talk about is the good ol' days and you have nothing to look forward to, you're near-sighted. If all you talk about is other people and what they're doing with their lives while yours is passing by, you're near-sighted.

If you want to go to the next level, you have to *see* the next level. You have to become far-sighted. You must take your eyes off of what's directly in front of you and start getting a vision of where you want to go in the future. You'll never leave where you are until you see where you'd rather be!

SPIRITUAL SIGHT

A vision is the ability to see what others cannot see. You need to visualize your dreams with great clarity. Actress Suzanne Somers said, "I have used visualization as a tool for a successful career for years. I see myself doing what it is I want, and I do not let go of this picture until it manifests."

God gave us two types of sight: physical sight and spiritual sight. Physical sight is the ability to see with your physical eyes what everyone else sees. Spiritual sight is the ability to see inside what nobody else can see. Not just using your imagination, but seeing it on the inside by visualizing it.

What is visualization? It's simply seeing the invisible. It is seeing with the eye of faith.

I love the story of the Australian sailing team that had never won the America's Cup. In 1983, the head coach of the team had a new idea. "Let's try this visualization stuff." So, he had a cassette tape made which included a narration of the Australian team beating the American team. This audio recording included statements of a commentator reporting the race live, play-by-play, as if on the air.

On the audio recording, the Australian team heard statements such as:
- "We're going around the last buoy."
- "We're gaining on the competition."
- "The Australians are taking the lead."
- "For the first time in history, Australia is sailing past the Americans."
- "Australia has won the America's Cup!" (And the crowd roars!)

It had sound effects in the background with the wind blowing, the waves beating, and the enormous shouts of victory from the cheering fans on the shore! This little cassette tape went on for about 20 minutes. The coach would instruct his team to visualize themselves beating the Americans while they listened. He made his team members listen to this tape twice a day, each day, for three years! Can you imagine? Well, after three years, they certainly could.

When race day finally approached, and the Australians were up against their American rivals, their attitude wasn't one of fear or dread. They weren't nervous or concerned. Their attitude was simply, "Not them again! How many times do we have to beat these guys?"[70]

They had an entirely new mindset because of visualization. As you can guess, Australia won the America's Cup! That's the power of visualizing your desired result on the inside before it shows up on the outside.

You cannot just arrive at success without seeing something beforehand. Legendary golfer, Jack Nicklaus said, "I never hit a shot, not even in practice, without having a sharp, in-focus picture of it in my head."

How do people discover their dreams? It really is quite simple. By dreaming! In John Maxwell's book *Put Your Dreams to the Test*, he shares what a Dallas architect told him, 'If you're an architect, you can't start building a project until you've finished it.'"[71] In other words, he has to imagine the entire project, visualize it in his mind, then draw it, before he ever picked up a hammer and nail. He saw the end and then he began.

God works the same way. He said in Isaiah 46:10, "I make known the end from the beginning" (NIV).

Look at the story of the Tower of Babel in Genesis 11:6. These were ungodly men trying to build a tower that could reach Heaven (before we had concrete mixers, cement trucks, cranes, and power tools). The Lord said of them, "Behold, they are one people and they have all one language; and this is only the beginning of what they will do, and now nothing they have imagined they can do will be impossible for them" (AMPC).

Let those words resonate in your heart: Nothing that they have imagined they can do will be impossible for them. How does it begin? With your imagination. Second Corinthians 4:18 says, "So we fix our eyes not on what is seen, but on what is unseen, since what is seen is temporary, but what is unseen is eternal" (NIV).

Imagine it is exactly five years from today. What is the year? How old are you? If you're married, how long have you been married? If you have children, how old will they be in five years? Now, let's pretend that you change absolutely nothing in your current routine. You drive the same car, live in the same place, look the exact same, handle your money the same way, save the same amount each year, do the same things, go to the same places. Nothing has changed other than five years passing. Are you happy? Are you satisfied? Do you feel fulfilled? Or do you feel frustrated? Do you feel that you have missed out on something more that God has for your life?

Now let's pretend that you can have anything. It's five years from today. Go ahead and add up your age again but describe what you want to see.

- Are you married?
- Do you have a baby?
- Are your kids in college?
- Are you working? Where? Are you enjoying getting up each day because you're passionate about your career?
- What do you look like? Do you have an image of what you want to look like physically? See yourself from head to toe. Are you fit, in shape, and feeling alive?
- What are you driving? What color is it? Can you see yourself in it?

- What is your financial condition like? Are you saving money consistently? How much do you have saved by now? What is that exact number? Are you satisfied with that?

- Where do you live? Is it the same house you live in now? Have you moved? Are you living in a different city or state or country? Where is it? Is it on the lake? Is it on a large piece of property? Or a condo in the city? Is it near the beach or the mountains?

- Where have you been? Have you traveled? Are you enjoying life and all there is to see? Have you been to Paris, France or Tokyo, Japan or Rome, Italy?

- What have you accomplished? Did you finish that article and submit it for the local newspaper? Did you get that degree? Did you start that catering business? Did you learn how to create your own website? Can you speak French or Spanish fluently now? Did you start that side job that's generating an extra $10,000 annually?

- Are you ministering? Are you teaching a class? Did you write your first book? Did you go on your first mission trip? Is your debt paid off?

- What does your ideal life look like five years from now?

What are some of those dreams you had when you were a child? What about when you first became an adult? Are you living the life you imagined? If not, why? What is stopping you? Why can't you go back and get that college degree? Five years from now, you could have it.

Why can't you take those flying lessons? Sign up for an evening or weekend class. Five years from now, you could be flying planes, earning a larger salary, making new friendships, exposing yourself to the world.

Have you always wanted to get your realtor's license and sell houses? Do it now. Five years from now you could be living a completely different lifestyle. What's stopping you?

No matter how big or how small the dream may seem, it's a dream. It's a goal, and it's a vision. And it's needed to keep you alive and living your life to the fullest! So, close your eyes and visualize where you see yourself five years from today.

2. Write it down.

**"Goals in writing are dreams
with deadlines."
- Brian Tracy**

In recent years, a handwritten note from pop icon Michael Jackson was found in his warehouse after he died in 2009. They discovered a 21-year-old Michael had scribbled his dreams on the back of a tour itinerary in 1979.

"I should be a totally [sic] different person. People should never think of me as the kid who sang ABC... I should be a new, incredible actor/singer/dancer that will shock the world. I will do no interviews. I will be magic. I will be a perfectionist, a researcher, a trainer, a masterer [sic]. I will be better than every great actor roped into one."

He made promises to himself that he would study the work of great entertainers to improve himself. He also wrote: "I will study and look back on the whole world of entertainment and perfect it, take it steps further from where the greats left off."[72] And that's exactly what he did.

He created a vision on paper and then lived it. Michael Jackson went down in history as the "King of Pop" as well as the "Most Awarded Recording Artist in the History of Pop Music."

Habakkuk 2:2 says clearly to "Write the vision and make it plain." This isn't difficult; however, what's easy to do is also easy not to do. It's as simple as picking up the closest pen to you right now, grabbing a notebook, and writing. Remember, you wouldn't start laying bricks having no idea what you're building, nor should you start going after a vision that you've never sketched out. Write it down.

Be specific about what you saw as you visualized your life five years from now. Don't be vague. Don't just write, "I want a lot of money over the next five years." Your mind doesn't know how to define "a lot" so it has nothing to aim towards. Vague goals produce vague results. Be specific. It could be, "I have $50,000 saved in the next five years." That means you need to start saving $10,000 each year or $834 each month or $192 each week.

Many people fail to receive because they are not clear on what they want. Put some serious thought into what you want. Don't rush through this. This is your life. This is how you will be remembered and described by the generations who live after you. What do you want them to say? That's what you need to write.

Knowing what you want and writing it out in clear, compelling detail is a vital key to success. It's not enough to think about what you want; you must commit to putting it in writing. Unfortunately, most people, including myself for my first 33 years, have no idea what they want. Mark Twain recognized this lack of clarity by saying, "I can teach anybody how to get what they want in life. The problem is I can't find anybody who can tell me what they truly want."

When you develop this habit of getting crystal clear on your ambitions, your goals, and your dreams for life, you will no longer be where you are today. Your life will improve by leaps and bounds.

In a *Huffington Post* article, Mary Morrissey writes, "If you just THINK about one of your goals or dreams, you're only using the right hemisphere of your brain, which is your imaginative center. But, if you think about something that you desire, and then write it down, you also tap into the power of your logic-based left hemisphere...And you send your consciousness and every cell of your body a signal that says, 'I want this, and I mean it!'" Morrissey continues, "Just the act of writing down your dreams and goals ignites an entirely new dimension of consciousness, ideas and productivity to the powerhouse that is your subconscious mind."[73]

I do not claim to truly understand the psychological reasons behind the "power of the pen" or why the right and left hemispheres of our brains respond to clearly written aspirations. I just know from experience, it works!

As a result, the act of writing down your dreams and goals enables you to see opportunities all around you that you would have ignored had you not written them down.

President of High Point University, Nido Qubein said, "Nothing can add more power to your life than concentrating all your energies on a limited set of targets."[74] By writing out your goals, these "targets" become embedded in your subconscious mind. You are designating a destination for your brain to start driving towards.

The sad reality is that 97% of American adults are trying to live their lives without clear, specific, written goals. Brian Tracy compares doing so to "setting off across an unknown country without a road map. You may get somewhere eventually, but it will take you much longer, and it is far more likely that you will get lost, and waste an enormous amount of time, than if you planned your trip carefully."[75]

Described as the top sales training expert in the world, Grant Cardone owns and operates four companies that generate nearly $100 million annually and has written his goals down on paper for years. He says, "It's great for staying focused and keeping you on track." However, Cardone wasn't always this successful. In fact, recovering from a life of drug addiction and no direction for his life, the night he returned home from drug rehab, he started writing his dreams and goals in order to get his life focused and on the path to his dreams.

When he started this habit 20 years ago, he wrote down, "I own 20 apartments or more." At the time, he hadn't even bought one apartment and didn't know anything about apartments or financing. "I was completely clueless," said Cardone, "I had no idea *how* I was going to accomplish the goal; still I wrote it down and looked at that vision every day for years." Almost five years later, he made a real-estate deal, for 48 units in Vista, California. "Boom!" shouted Cardone, "A goal I had been obsessed with was achieved." Since then, he writes his goals down faithfully every morning and every night.[76]

This is a clear habit of the most successful people in the world no matter what age. Even a young kid named Caleb Maddix started reading success books at six years old by the recommendation of his father. Like we read about John Maxwell's dad, Caleb's dad wouldn't agree to pay him to do normal household chores like other kids, but he volunteered to pay his son $20 for each book he read about success. Caleb eagerly agreed.

By age eight, Caleb's dad had him start writing his goals. They included:

- I will speak with Gary V. (Gary Vaynerchuk)!
- I will do a Ted Talk.
- I will do an event with Tony Robbins.
- I will make $100k by 14.
- I will have 100k followers on Facebook.

Everything he wrote down has happened. Last I heard, he was on target to make $1 million dollars by age 16, which was another dream he wrote down.[77]

When the vision is clear, the results will appear.

TOP TEN

Being clear about your goals and objectives will help you focus and stay on track. I recommend writing your top 10 goals for the year by acting as if it's December 31st. Act as if your greatest goals have been achieved by New Year's Eve, and you enthusiastically declare to your friends, "This has been the most amazing year of my life!" What needs to happen for you to say that? Write them out in the past tense to help you "act as if" it's already been accomplished.

It could be:

- We paid off our $3,000 VISA bill.
- My student loan of $11,000 was paid in full!
- We went on a weekend getaway to New York City for $3,000.
- I sold my first house as a realtor.
- I reached my goal weight of 125 lbs, and I'm maintaining it.
- We saved $5,000.
- I finished my manuscript, and it's going to print.
- I read 12 books.

Brian Tracy recommends what I've done for years. Write your top 10 goals down in a notebook for 30 solid days without skipping a day and without looking back to the previous day to see what you wrote. In other words, if you can't remember all 10 on day two, it's okay. Perhaps all 10 weren't as important to you. Just write the goals you remember each day, for a full month.

The reason behind this daily practice, as Tracy explains, is that it causes your goals to become so ingrained in your subconscious mind that you become more determined than ever to truly go after them and enjoy the thrill of checking them off.

Clarity is one of the single most important keys to success. You will be amazed at what you can accomplish in life when you get crystal clear on where you are going!

3. Make a vision board or vision book.

In an interview with Oprah, Steve Harvey explained why he's committed to having vision boards. "Man, if I didn't have no vision board, I'd be in trouble," said Harvey. "You gotta keep it in front of you. It's on my laptop. It's on my screen on my phone. It's on my iPad. It's on my desktop."[78]

> **"You've got to create dream boards.**
> **You've got to put the new car up. Put**
> **the weight you want to be. If you can**
> **see it in your mind, you can hold it**
> **in your hand."**
> **- Steve Harvey**

Fascinated by Harvey's dedication to vision boards, Oprah explained that 10 years earlier, she had entire shows talking about vision boards, but skeptics came out against her saying, "That doesn't work." She pointed to Harvey in their interview, emphatically saying, "You are living proof. It absolutely does (work)." Oprah admonished, "You have to have a vision and a plan to execute so that every step moves you in the direction of vision."

When Oprah asked Harvey what types of things he had on his vision board, he said people would laugh at how big some of his visions were. Some of his dreams included personally paying for 10,000 children to attend college, discovering new ways to build the infrastructure for trade in Africa, what type of plane he wants to own, etc.

But Harvey's dreams aren't only on a board or a screen. He takes it a step further by having his tailor sew some of his most important dreams inside the hem of his suit pants. That's how dedicated he is to keep his dreams and goals with him at all times, in front of him, around him, even on him.

Do what you need to do to keep your vision in front of you continually.

The more vivid a picture you paint of where you want to go, the more decisive you will become! You might wonder, *Is it really that important to mess around with adding pictures to a vision board or book?* I am telling you from experience, it's worth the effort. Your mind thinks in pictures, not in words.

Have you ever seen a young boy who's really into football or basketball and his whole bedroom is covered with pictures of his heroes and sports memorabilia? He is surrounding himself with what he wants. That's vision.

I read where actress Emma Stone went against all odds to pursue her dream of acting by creating a vision for her parents to see. She had to get crystal clear and convince them that moving to Hollywood was the best thing for their family so she could become a star. How? By showing them her dream in clear, compelling details.

She created a PowerPoint presentation about why she should pursue a career in acting, naming it "Project Hollywood" and even playing Madonna's single "Hollywood" as the presentation's soundtrack. How could any parent refuse such a creative and well-thought out proposition? Yes, Stone's mother packed her bags and accompanied her to Tinseltown (Hollywood).[79] Stone was only 15 years old at the time, and today she is an Academy Award winning actress. That's the power of seeing your vision before your eyes.

Singer/Rapper Drake told *Rolling Stone Magazine* how he obtained his dream home. "This house was the desktop image on my computer for years," Drake says. "I was like, 'What are the world's craziest residential pools?' and when I searched online, this came up." His research was done in 2007. At the time he was googling outrageous swimming pools to enlarge his ability to dream, he was an unsigned artist. He wasn't loaded. He wasn't ready to purchase a mansion in Beverly Hills. However, that didn't stop him from getting a vision and keeping it before his eyes.

In 2009, the house hit the market with an asking price of $27 million. A few years later, the owner of Drake's ideal home and picturesque swimming pool "was at a low moment," Drake recalls. "He needed money." In 2012, Drake bought the property for $7.7 million. "I stole it from him!" he says.[80]

Let that sink in; only five years earlier, he researched his dream property with no means to obtain it. But he was "far-sighted," seeing where he was headed rather than "near-sighted" by the current impossibility. He kept the vision before him on a computer screen and five years later, he was living in it.

Find a photo of your dream house, your ideal body, your perfect vacation. Superimpose your photo on the cover of a book, a magazine, or a newspaper. Get pictures of the bedroom furniture you desire, the wedding ring you love, and the car you want to drive. Find photos that match each of your dreams and have fun with this. Instead of always framing your past with the graduation photos, the family vacation from 20 years ago, and the wedding pictures from 1991, why not frame your future. Showcase where you believe God is taking your life. It's exciting. It's compelling, and it drives you to not settle where you are but rather long for where you want to be.

THE LAW OF ATTRACTION

Fix your eyes on your vision board. The Law of Attraction basically states that whatever you focus on, you will attract in your life. Proverbs 23:7 says it this way, "For as he thinketh in his heart, so is he" (KJV). What you think about, you bring about. When you look at pictures of where you're headed, it gets planted into your subconscious mind, and your subconscious doesn't know any different than to make it happen.

Is it a coincidence that once I started writing my dreams and goals, then adding pictures to illustrate them, reviewing them daily, they started happening? Not one bit. I'm talking about specific dreams:

- Be the keynote speaker at the Amway conference.

- Minister at the largest church in France.
- See my books in the *7ici Librairie Chrétienne* bookstore in Paris.
- Motivate and minister to the Dallas Cowboys Cheerleaders.
- Have offices on the lake in Rockwall, Texas.
- Meet Oprah Winfrey.
- Get invited to the White House.

Everything on my vision board years ago is a reality today. So, I keep designing new ones. When you design a vision board or even a vision book (by placing your photos in a spiral notebook), you are literally surrounding yourself with what can be…not just what is. You are framing your future.

Like Steve Harvey said, "You gotta keep it in front of you." Don't put all this work into your vision only to keep it in a desk drawer or nightstand to be viewed on New Year's Day. We move towards what we consistently see. Keep it in front of your eyes.

What should you put on your vision board? Anything that inspires and motivates you. (My book, *Dream It. Pin It. Live It.*, walks you through making a vision board in detail.) Add visual goals for the following areas: relationships, career, finances, health, home, travel, personal growth, and whatever dream you have in your heart. You want to keep your goals out of reach but never out of sight. Keep your vision board in sight at all times. When you look at your most important goals and your big vision, your motivation goes to a whole new level.

4. Take action.

**"Take action! An inch of movement
will bring you closer to your goals
than a mile of intention."
- Steve Maraboli**

What do you do while you're waiting for your dreams to unfold?

Yes, you are visualizing consistently. You've written your dreams and goals. You've added images to each desire, and you are keeping it before your eyes. Now what? Our handbook for success (the Bible) clearly says, "Faith without works (corresponding action) is dead" (James 2:17, NKJV). Now, you have to add feet to your dreams.

I never want to give the impression that I just make a cute, little collage of photos of ministering in Paris, driving a Porsche, living on the lake, and poof! They just happen! No, I've had to get up and go after each dream on that board.

Jack Canfield said, "The one thing that seems to separate winners from losers more than anything else is this: Winners take action."[81] They know their dream will require work, demand persistence, and involve challenges, but they refuse to give up! They're so compelled by their clear vision that they fight for their dreams.

Sarah Jessica Parker did just that. The Oscar winning actress was born in Ohio by parents who divorced when she was young. Riddled with poverty, she grew up wearing 99 cent dresses and sharing clothes with her seven siblings. She was accustomed to living with little to nothing, surviving on welfare with bill collectors calling and the phone company shutting off the phones. At times they endured winter with no electricity and no presents to celebrate Christmas. "We were all old enough to either get the calls or watch my mother's reactions shuffling the money around." She said. "There was no great way to hide being poor."

Rather than focus on all the obstacles that could prevent her from her dream, Sarah Jessica Parker began looking for opportunities to change the direction of her life and ultimately change her family's legacy.

This little girl with no advantages or favor on her side took action. She practiced singing and studied ballet. The family picked up and moved from Cincinnati, Ohio to New York City to see what was available for her. She would wake up early in the mornings to go to the theater, the ballet, and the opera when they offered free tickets for children on weekends. She practiced and studied and seized opportunities to improve her craft.

At 12 years old, she auditioned for Broadway and was cast for the title role in the legendary play, *Annie*, acting alongside the one and only Bob Hope in 1979. One break led to another and that little girl rose from severe poverty to sitcom sensation as the shoe-loving Carrie Bradshaw on a HBO hit show. Her net worth is now over $100 million.[82]

BEHIND THE SCENES

What do you need to do in order to take action? We've discussed thoroughly throughout this book that you can't be powerful in public but pitiful in private. What you do behind the scenes is all preparation for where God wants to take you. Think of the hours Sarah Jessica Parker practiced her ballet poses, her dance moves, her voice lessons, and her lines to memorize. Nobody saw that little girl putting in the effort behind the scenes.

Every single day is another opportunity to take action. What does that mean to you personally?
- Write another chapter.
- Get your resume typed.
- Join the gym.
- Get your passport.
- Save $100 from this week's paycheck.
- Register online.
- Apply for a scholarship.
- Test drive the car.
- Research the business.
- Enroll in the class.

- Start the lessons.
- Call a mentor.
- Schedule a meeting.
- Go on a trip.

John Maxwell says, "There's a price to pay for success. However, if you continue to complain about the price; you'll eventually stop paying it."[83] Every successful person has put in the hours and taken the necessary—sometimes painful—steps to achieve their dreams. You can do this.

WHEN JESUS SAW THEIR FAITH

I've discovered Jesus wants to *see* your faith. In fact, there's a story in Luke 5 of four friends who took their seriously ill friend to Jesus in hopes of seeing him healed. In desperate need of a miracle, they carried their friend on a stretcher to the place where Jesus was ministering, but when they arrived, the venue was filled to capacity. There was no hope of getting inside. It looked like all their effort of trekking across town carrying a full-grown man on a stretcher was for nothing. The door was closed. The opportunity was missed. In other words, it must not have been God's will for him to be healed or there would have been room for them to squeeze inside.

No. That was not their attitude for one minute. Just because a door is closed doesn't mean it's not God's will. Sometimes you have to go through a window. If the window is closed, you may have to climb on top of a house, tear off the shingles, and climb through the roof! Do what you need to do to see your dream achieved. That's what these four guys did. They stopped at nothing!

Suddenly, in the middle of his sermon, Jesus saw four guys above him, lowering their friend through the ceiling, on a stretcher, down to where he was standing. The Bible says, "When Jesus saw their faith..."

Let me point out that faith is invisible, so what exactly could Jesus see? Their action. He saw that they were willing to go the extra mile, do whatever it takes, to see their dream come true.

The Bible goes on to say, "When Jesus saw their faith, he said, 'Friend, your sins are forgiven.'" And He healed the man. The four friends got their dream, although it required doing more than what most would be willing to do.

Take action. Jesus sees when you get away by yourself and start visualizing the possibilities for your life. You begin pondering, asking Him to speak to you, listening quietly for any direction He gives. Then, you pick up a pen and some paper to begin writing every far-fetched, crazy, wild dream that comes in your heart. You take it a step further by causing the images in your head to become physical photos on a board. Then, you see your potential in front of you and begin listing action steps to get you closer…I am convinced that when Jesus sees your faith (your action), your dream is closer than you think.

List out possible action steps you can start taking for each of your dreams and goals. Push yourself out of your place of comfort knowing that each time you do, you're getting closer. You're growing. You're learning. You're building your confidence.

Comfort and convenience run the lives of unsuccessful people. Successful people are always doing things that make them uncomfortable. The men and women in the Bible who literally changed the world were constantly taking big steps of faith outside their comfort zone! Peter walked on water. The lady with the issue of blood faced the crowd when she wasn't allowed to be in public. The widow woman gave the prophet her last bit of food. What do you need to do that makes you a little nervous, uncomfortable, awkward, and stretched? Do it.

It could be that you need to go to a conference alone, go to dinner with someone who makes quite a bit more money than you, send your manuscript to an agent or publisher, agree to do an interview or speak at an event, host a small group at your house, invite someone famous to speak at your event or church, sign up for a class, enroll at your local gym, agree to sing at the concert, sign up for a 5k, get your business cards printed. Whatever it is, push yourself. Do it.

The distance between your dreams and reality is called action.

5. Believe.

> **"The future belongs to those who**
> **believe in the beauty of their dreams."**
> **- Eleanor Roosevelt**

If your dreams are possible, you're not dreaming big enough. If they were possible, they wouldn't require faith, and it's impossible to please God without faith (Hebrews 11:6). Anything God is telling you to do is going to seem outside the realm of possibility. I've never had one dream look reasonable when God first gave it to me. Each of the dreams and goals that I have written in my notebook look so far-fetched that it often feels ridiculous, but that's just it. God wants our total dependency, our faith, and our complete trust in Him to see these dreams accomplished.

In order to achieve anything in your life, you must believe. You may recall the story of Abraham being told by God that he would be the Father of many nations. Considering that Abraham was impotent by that time in his life, and his wife, Sarah, had already undergone the change of life, it was what some would label "unbelievable." However, the Bible says, "When there was nothing left to hope for, Abraham still hoped and *believed*. As a result, he became a father of many nations, as he had been told'" (Romans 4:18, GW emphasis added).

He hoped, he believed, and he became.

So how do you demonstrate that you believe? What do you do after you've visualized your dreams, written them out clearly, added images depicting your aspirations, and even started taking some strategic steps towards them?

The greatest tool God has given you to demonstrate your belief is right under your nose. It's with the words of your mouth. You release your faith by speaking to your dreams. Simply speak what you believe and believe what you speak.

> **"Since we have the same spirit of faith, according to what has been written, 'I believed, and therefore I spoke,' we also believe, and therefore speak..."**
> **- 2 Corinthians 4:13–14, NKJV**

I wrote an entire book on the language of success called *Pep Talk*, in which I explain that God created the entire world with the words of His mouth. In like manner, you create your world with the words coming out of your mouth. As we discussed in Chapter 5, the most successful people in the world practice the art of making positive affirmations and speaking to their dreams.

When outward appearances look contrary to the dreams on your vision board, when your circumstances are tragic, trying, and draining you of emotional strength, that's when you need to declare with even more fervency, "I believe!"

God's Word says that death and life are in the power of the tongue (Proverbs 18:21, NKJV). You're speaking either death or life to your dreams each time you voice your thoughts. Which will you choose? It may look like your dreams will never happen...but don't speak it. It may look like it's going to take years to achieve...but don't speak it. It may appear that nothing is working in your favor...but don't speak it! If you want to know where your life is headed, listen to the words coming out of your mouth.

Words are powerful. Whatever you are speaking is what you're currently manifesting in your life. Speak to your dreams. Just as God commanded Ezekiel to speak to a valley of dry bones and command them to come to life (Ezekiel 37), you have to speak to your seemingly dead dreams to see them resurrected.

I have discovered that the highest expression of your faith in God is gratitude for what He is about to do in your life. That's extreme faith. When you go ahead and say, "Thank You, Lord," for something that hasn't even manifested, that's radical belief.

THE CHECK IS IN THE MAIL

In the early days of my Icing Women's Conference, a friend of mine called my office and spoke with my assistant, Donna. He expressed that he was so touched by our outreach to young women, rescuing them from human trafficking and giving them tools to help them on a path to success, that he wanted to completely underwrite the budget of our next Icing event.

Immediately, Donna called me to share this extraordinary news. Since I was driving, I almost had to pull over on the side of the road in complete shock. I said, "What? He's going to pay for the whole event?"

She said, "Yes! He asked me for the budget, I told him, and he's sending a check."

I shouted, "Thank You, Jesus!" I asked Donna for his phone number so I could personally thank him and had her send him a Bundt cake with a note that read, "You're nothing bundt the best. Thank you for helping us spread Icing." (I love puns!)

As soon as we hung up, I called my friend and profusely thanked him for being so generous, and I prayed that God would multiply his significant seed into our ministry and bless him just as extravagantly.

Now, think about it. My response to my friend doesn't seem so fanatical, does it? Don't you normally thank people who do nice things for you? But here's my point: I thanked my friend, and I even sent him a gift of gratitude *before* I ever saw the check. Why? I had faith in his word. I trusted him. I knew him. I thoroughly believed he would do what he said he would do, so I went ahead and told him how much I appreciated it.

Well, God is not a man that he should lie. He already said:

- "No good thing will He withhold from those who walk uprightly" (Psalm 84:11, NKJV).
- "Delight yourself in the Lord, and he will give you the desires of your heart" (Psalm 37:4, ESV).
- "Truly, I tell you, if anyone says to this mountain, 'Go, throw yourself into the sea,' and does not doubt in their heart but believes that what they say will happen, it will be done for them. Therefore I tell you, whatever you ask for in prayer, believe that you have received it, and it will be yours" (Mark 11:23–24, NIV).

Go ahead and thank Him for what you believe He is about to do in your life. Act as if the check is in the mail! I'm so convinced in the importance of expressing gratitude before your breakthrough that my friends often think it has already happened. Many times, I've been walking down the streets of Paris with my ministry team and said (with squeals in my voice and a ridiculous smile across my face), "Thank You, Jesus, for my gorgeous Parisian apartment! I am sooooo grateful!" I have had women say, "Oh my gosh, congratulations! That's incredible. When did you get your apartment?" I reply, "Not yet...it's on its way though!"

Denzel Washington said, "Say thank you in advance for what's already yours. That's how I live my life. That's one of the reasons I am where I am today."[84] A grateful heart is a magnet for miracles. When you're grateful, you attract more to be grateful for.

It's a Personal Habit

As I routinely go through my five habits each morning, I simply look at my vision board and speak my dreams out loud, thanking the Lord ahead of time for what He is about to do in my life. Many successful people write their goals down every single day as part of their ritual. I, however, only do this in the month of January, where I write them down every day for 30 days. For the remainder of the year, I give life to my dreams by speaking to them and expressing gratitude to God for what He is about to do.

Whatever makes your dreams come alive and stay alive as you're waiting for them to manifest, do it. Speak them out. Write them down. Review them. Make it personal to and for you.

One thing is for certain, if you keep your dreams in your head, they'll forever remain dreams. When you pencil your dreams, it sets the course of your life down a path to success. Earl Nightingale, the father of personal growth, asked the questions, "Is there a key to becoming successful? Why do so many people work so hard and never achieve anything? Why do some people seem to have everything they touch turn to gold? It's because of goals! People with goals succeed because they know where they are going."

MY DAILY ROUTINE

Pam Winters
Founder of Leadership Team Development
Daily 5:

1. Quiet time, praise and worship.

2. Review calendar and schedule to be sure I am prepared and organized, prioritize tasks, look over dreams and goals.

3. Some type of exercise.

4. Listen to teaching audio.

5. Read in a success book or listen to a book on audio.

7

HOW TO START (AND MAINTAIN) A FIT LIFESTYLE

HABIT #5: EXERCISE

Successful people exercise. Most have either run a couple miles, swam a few laps or climbed a few floors before others have even had their bowl of cereal in the morning. Everyone from Lady Gaga, Mark Cuban, Cher, Mick Jagger, and Jennifer Aniston consider morning exercise integral to their success. Whether it's a round of golf, a tennis match, a yoga session, or a trip to the gym, exercise gives you a massive boost of energy to propel you all day.

Whatever your reason for exercise, to lose weight for a special occasion or to get that 'revenge body' to make your ex wish they'd never let you go, people who exercise for *health reasons* are more likely to make it a lifestyle than those who do so only for appearance. Successful people exercise because it helps them be their best.

Vogue editor-in-chief, Anna Wintour plays a game of tennis at the crack of dawn each day. Apple CEO, Tim Cook heads to the gym at 5 a.m. every morning and has done so for years. GoPro founder and CEO, Nick Woodman surfs the waves, snowboards, and enjoys mountain biking consistently. Former PepsiCo CEO, Steve Reinemund runs four miles every morning at 5:00 a.m. Kohl's CEO, Michelle Gass wakes up each morning at 4:30 a.m. to go running.[85] Exercise not only keeps your physical body in shape, but it keeps your mind sharp.

These success moguls aren't necessarily trying to get bikini-ready or become competitive bodybuilders. They desire to be fit inside and out to tackle their most important challenges. They give their body the attention it deserves because it affects their overall well-being. Physical health affects your emotional and mental health.

Americans spend $60+ billion dollars each year trying to lose weight. Look at this breakdown of money spent in 2010:

- Diet soft drinks – $21.15 billion
- Health clubs (Gym statistics: members, equipment, and cancellations) – $19.5 billion
- Medical plans (prescription diet drugs, hospital or physician plans, low calorie plans) – $8.25 billion
- Bariatric surgery – $5.77 billion
- Commercial weight loss centers – $3.29 billion
- Meal replacements and diet pills – $2.69 billion
- Artificial sweeteners – $2.52 billion
- Low calorie/diet foods – $2.32 billion
- Diet books and exercise videos – $1.21 billion[86]

After all this money is spent trying to lose weight and get in shape, nearly all dieters (90-95%) regain the weight they lost within one to five years.[87] I promise I'm going to motivate you with this chapter, not depress you. Please keep reading!

Each year, more and more people are trying to get their bodies in shape and their weight under control so why are nearly all dieters gaining their weight (and even more) right back? A report showed that adults who have gone on yo-yo diets for most of their lives (losing weight and gaining weight repeatedly) have lost an average of 270 lbs in their lifetime before successfully losing weight and keeping it off.[88]

It sounds crazy, doesn't it? Those 5–10 pounds that we gain and lose and gain and lose add up. The typical American dieter makes a New Year's resolution to lose weight and continues to make that announcement at least four times throughout the year without success.

Here's the truth: resolutions and diets don't work. We have proven that. Statistics show that nearly half of all New Year's resolutions are broken by February. They don't even make it through the second month of the year. Within two weeks, nearly 1/4 of resolutions are broken. Within three weeks, 1/3 of resolutions are broken. And within one month, nearly 1/2 of resolutions are forgotten. What is the answer? You know by now, as with anything else we want in life, it must become a habit.

Instead of resolving to lose weight on January 1st, I want you to see exercise as something you automatically do each day without even blinking. It's like getting dressed each morning. It's just what you do. Why? Because you have a new mindset. You are on a path to success. You are joining the ranks of the most successful people in the world who invest in their physical bodies. You're not the person you used to be. You desire to be the best possible version of yourself.

The Physical and Emotional Link

I want you to know that being in shape and investing in yourself physically doesn't mean you have to be a size zero (ladies) or a Greek god (men); it just means you commit to some sort of daily activity to keep your mind sharp, your body fit, and your energy at its peak. You give energy to gain energy for your dreams.

Let me explain to you how this vital habit became (and lasted all these years) part of my daily five. We all know that exercise is good for us. It keeps your weight in balance, makes you stronger, and keeps you feeling youthful and active as you age, but did you know that exercise also effects your emotional state? As you've followed along my journey from 2002 until today, you recall the former miserable person I was on the verge of a divorce, lonely, insecure, visionless, and just surviving until I made my list of five things I would practice every day for 21 days. Endeavoring to start new habits in my life, I was determined to stick with these disciplines for three solid weeks with no exception.

As we've thoroughly discussed in the previous chapters, my list included:

1. Pray and meditate
2. Read
3. Listen to faith-building/motivational messages
4. Write and review my dreams and goals
5. Exercise

In high school and college, I'd been disciplined in my exercise routine, but it had become more sporadic through the years. I would start a workout program to hit a big goal like summer vacation. I would be consistent about walking every day for one solid hour, lose the weight I wanted to lose for vacation, and never work out again for another nine months.

When my life hit that all-time low, I was desperate for major changes in every area of my life. I discovered (from habits #2 and #3: reading and listening) that there is a link between physical health and emotional health. A simple walk outside in the fresh air can bring a series of health benefits to your overall well-being. Well, I needed a complete overhaul! Numerous research has shown that exercise is one of the most important habits you can develop to completely transform your life. And you don't have to invest a lot of time doing it to see the benefits. So, I was determined to go all-in on this new discipline.

At that time in my life, I wasn't overweight. In fact, quite the opposite, I was malnourished. I had an extremely poor diet. It consisted of eating a bean and cheese burrito, nachos, and an extra-large sweet tea almost daily. But hardly anything else the rest of the day other than peanut butter crackers or maybe a Snickers bar. I'm serious. I would practically starve myself all day and then the big reward was eating my favorite meal: cheap, Mexican fast food.

That first morning the alarm sounded at 4:45 a.m. I pushed snooze, then fifteen minutes later, I got up at 5:00 a.m., slipped on my jogging shoes, added a little mascara (I just have to!), and went outside in the pitch dark. At first, I was a little creeped out by the darkness in my neighborhood at that hour. Even with the street lights still on, I could barely see my hand in front of my face. With my cell phone in my pocket and a can of pepper spray in my right hand, I began walking towards the stop sign at the end of my street.

The neighborhood was so quiet I could almost hear my own thoughts. There weren't any kids playing, any cars starting up or any birds chirping; it was just me on a lonely, quiet, dark street in Crowley, Texas with nothing to look at but the stars above me. It went from a little creepy to incredibly peaceful. As I rounded the end of the street and headed back towards my house to conclude lap number one, I began praying in my own head (not out loud in case another walker was behind me and thought I was nuts).

I talked to the Lord about what was on my heart, the pain I was feeling, the confusion I was having, the mess I was in. I told Him everything. I held nothing back. I mean, He already knew, but it felt good getting it all out. Somehow, even though I couldn't hear Him responding back to me like my best friend, Theresa, does, I knew He was intently listening. The more I talked, the more I forgot how many laps I had done. Before I knew it, my alarm went off, and I had been walking and talking with the Lord for one full hour. It felt like fifteen minutes. I had to go inside and start getting my little girl ready for school, but I could hardly wait for another "appointment" with my new best friend the next day.

I eagerly crossed off day number one of exercise on my wall calendar. Again, I did it the next day and the next day. What I thought would be a massive chore or drudgery to keep my commitment became what I most looked forward to each day. I could hardly wait to get up and start my day with another free therapy session. At the end of 21 days, I couldn't imagine stopping this counseling appointment. I was gaining such clarity about my life, my personality, my weaknesses, my insecurities all from a simple commitment to walk up and down my street each day before the sun rose.

My walk with the Lord opened a whole new world to me. I drew closer to Him than I had ever been in my entire life. In addition to hearing His voice and understanding myself better, I gained a multitude of benefits because of this discipline. I was sleeping better. I started taking vitamins. I began drinking water instead of sweet tea with every meal. I gradually chose a salad over a burrito. My anxiety was lifting. My mind was sharper. And as a bonus, my body looked better than ever. Why would I even consider stopping something that provided a wealth of benefits? And that's exactly why it's still a part of my daily five.

I mentioned previously how Charles Duhigg explains in his bestselling book, *The Power of Habit*, how once we establish certain keystone habits, they lead to other good habits. Exercise is a keystone, foundational habit, that will lead you to adopting many life-changing patterns for improvement, which is exactly what happened with me. I had no idea that nearly two decades later, I would still be lacing up my shoes at 5:00 in the morning. This habit has given me the stamina to do what I am doing today: traveling to Europe this month to speak 14 times, appear on two interviews, record four podcasts, and write this book all within 28 days while traveling between four countries. Exercise is vital to your success.

First, we have to be convinced of the benefits of exercising and equally aware of the consequences of not. Then, we must eliminate any excuse preventing us from caring about our health and make it a part of our daily routine like making our bed. (You do make your bed each day, right? It's also part of the habits of successful people!)

You must determine why exercise is important to you. Maybe your pants have gotten too tight or you want to compete in a fitness competition. Maybe you saw a photo of yourself overweight and it was humiliating enough to make a change. Perhaps you had a family member die of a disease that could have been prevented had they exercised. Or maybe you feel so drained of energy each day and are desperate to have that zeal again to jump out of bed in the morning.

It's hard to commit to a new habit that isn't meaningful to you, so I wanted to point out a few benefits of working out as well as a few consequences to not exercising and show you how much the commitment outweighs the excuse.

5 Benefits of Exercise

1. Exercise makes you happier.

Most people who don't work out think of exercise as depressing, dreadful, torture; but those who do work out, find it fulfilling and it makes them happier. It has been scientifically proven to release certain chemicals such as Dopamine into your brain that cause you to be joyful. As we age, studies suggest that we are constantly losing levels of Dopamine, and the way we generate more is through exercise. Who knew that jumping rope or playing badminton with your kids can scientifically make you more pleasant to be around and happier?

2. Exercise makes you sleep better.

You can trade your bottle of sleeping pills for some new jogging shoes. Physical activity has been shown to help reduce insomnia and provide quality sleep as well as giving you the pep in your step to wake up more energetic about the day ahead. Who doesn't want more sound sleep?

3. Exercise reduces stress.

Seven out of ten adults in the U.S. say they experience stress or anxiety daily.[89] Physicians consistently recommend exercise to reduce mental fatigue, combat anxiety, and lessen stress. They know if your body feels better, so does your mind. Taking the dog for a walk or cycling around your block can help you release negative emotions such as fear, anger, worry, and improve your overall mood. If anyone should know about stress, it would be a man who owns 400 companies. Yet when Richard Branson was asked how he stays productive and stress-free, the wealthiest man in the U.K. answered, "I work out."[90]

4. Exercise gives you a boost of energy.

I find it ironic how the same thing people who don't exercise complain about—a lack of energy—is the very thing produced by exercising. No matter how exhausted you feel, when you muster the willpower to go work out, it *energizes* you. You actually feel more energized after you work out than you did before it. Facebook CEO, Mark Zuckerberg, who works out at least three times a week first thing in the morning said, "Doing anything well requires energy, and you just have a lot more energy when you're fit."[91]

5. Exercise builds your confidence.

Looking good makes you feel good. When you don't feel confident about how you look, it leads to a poor self-image, low self-esteem, and insecurity. That effects every part of your life: the career you choose, the relationships you pursue, your prayer life, and even the goals and dreams you feel qualified to go after. Confidence is attractive. As your body improves, your mindset improves. You will not only look and feel better, but your emotional health will rise and build your confidence from the inside out.

5 Consequences of Not Exercising

Once you see some of the biggest effects of not exercising, your perspective will shift, and you will become more inspired than ever to look for opportunities to incorporate a little activity each day.

1. Lack of exercise results in early death.

This medically proven consequence alone should be enough proof for us to go dust off the old roller blades and at least, make a lap around the block. Yet, an alarming 1 out of every 10 premature deaths around the planet are caused by not exercising (almost as much as smoking). The American Heart Association reports that approximately 250,000 deaths every year are caused by not exercising.

2. Lack of exercise results in higher risk for depression.

The *American Journal of Preventive Medicine* reviewed 30 large studies on depression discovering that 25 of those studies confirmed people who don't exercise have a higher risk of depression and mood disorders. There is a link between emotional health and physical health.

3. Lack of exercise leads to sickness.

Without regular exercise, you have a higher risk of heart disease, diabetes, colon cancer, and high blood pressure. In addition to these major illnesses, a lack of physical activity results in catching the flu or a cold more often. There are even reports that exercise increases how quickly your white blood cells work. This means exercise may prevent some sickness-causing bacteria or even flush bacteria out of your body quicker.

4. Lack of exercise leads to aging faster.

Nobody wants that! Without exercise, your muscles and bones grow weak. When it comes to scientifically measuring the rate of aging, a study by the Arthritis Foundation found that people who don't do strength training may age faster than people who do. Weight-bearing or resistance training exercises has been reported to help preserve bone density, while the lack thereof increases the risk of osteoporosis and fractures as you get older. Aging adults who disregard exercise are more likely to fall than those who work out, which only makes sense because their body is stronger.

5. Lack of exercise leads to being overweight or obese.

This is an obvious one, yet it's still not motivating enough to get 80% of people off the couch and out the door. Not exercising and being overweight increases the risk of diabetes, heart disease, stroke as well as breast, cervical, endometrial, and liver cancer in women; and prostate, colon, and rectal cancer in men.[92]

Stop Making Excuses

Obviously, this is not an exhaustive list of all the benefits exercise gives you, nor all the consequences a lack of exercise results in, but hopefully, it's enough to make you grab a jump rope or throw a Frisbee in the back yard with your dog.

The truth is that we may never *feel* like exercising, just as we may never feel like brushing our teeth. That's why we must make it a habit. You must push your feelings aside, give yourself a pep talk, and make it a part of your daily five if you want to become a person of discipline. Once you stop making excuses for why you can't do it and start focusing on why you must make it happen, it will affect all other aspects of your life in positive ways.

MY DAILY ROUTINE

Elena Serda
President of Elena C Serda Consulting Services
Daily 5:

1. The first thing I do before my feet hit the floor is meditate and pray.

2. I say daily affirmations and acknowledge the things I am grateful for.

3. I work out 4-6 days a week.

4. Daily I listen to faith and business messages.

5. I intentionally set goals for the day and reflect on my aspirations.

Making Exercise a Habit

An overwhelming majority of Americans, at least 45 million, are on a diet at any given time. At the same time, the Centers for Disease Control and Prevention reports that 68% of people over the age of 20 are either obese or overweight. Unfortunately, nearly 65% of those who put in the hard work to lose weight will return right back to their pre-dieting weight within three years.

It gets even worse for those who go on a crash diet to lose weight fast. Only 5% of those who work hard to lose weight rapidly will keep the weight off. Think about that. Ninety-five percent will go right back to where they were before the diet. Because they don't make it a habit.[93]

The key to being in shape, feeling better, and maintaining your fitness goals is to make it a habit. So, let's get started with this new discipline.

1. Visualize your ideal body.

> **"Whatever the mind can conceive and believe, it can achieve."**
> **- Napoleon Hill**

Everything begins with vision. The statistics above prove that if you don't first have a clear vision of how you want to look and feel, and a compelling reason why it's important to you, you're unlikely to stay committed.

We are bombarded with images of people who have perfect bodies that require hours each day in the gym, protein powders, raw eggs, and a spray tan. However, I want *you* to decide what *you* want to look like at *your* best. Yes, we all have parts we wish were better, no matter how disciplined we are with exercise, but don't let that stop you from getting a vision of you at your best self (no matter what the number is on the scale or the size is on the clothing rack).

Close your eyes and imagine looking in the mirror and seeing a fit and healthier version of you. Imagine you truly love what you see. You are full of energy, enthusiastic about life, and you enjoy trying on new clothes because you feel good in your skin. I mean truly imagine being 100% content with your body. I'm not saying you're perfect, but you're perfectly happy with yourself.

What is that ideal picture? Whatever it is for you, put that image on your vision board or inside your vision book and look at it *daily*. It could be a younger version of you (from an old photo) or a picture of someone you admire. If so, put your head on top of their body and imagine that's your physique. Don't laugh! It works. Think about it, how do you know if you've achieved a fitness goal if you don't know what your goal looks like? Remember, these photos should inspire you, not bring you down.

When you feel depleted of energy, look at your vision. When you don't see any changes, look at your vision. When you feel like giving up on this habit, look at your vision. When you're struggling to find the motivation to get going, look at your future self and go!

2. Develop your unique plan.

To stay committed to this discipline, you have to find what works for you specifically. If you're forcing yourself out of bed each morning but you loathe what you're doing, your commitment won't last. You need to find an activity you enjoy.

I mentioned how I began my lifestyle of exercising daily by walking in the early mornings up and down my street. It became something I was eager to get up and go do because of the peace it brought as I communicated with the Lord in prayer. I was so desperate for peace in that season of my life, so when I found it, I instantly connected exercising with joy.

Today, my morning workouts consist of going to a gym for 30 minutes of weight training and 30 minutes of cardio. When I'm traveling, I always take a resistance band with me to use in the hotel rooms in case I don't have access to a gym.

For you, it could be riding bikes with your children or mate. It could be walking around the soccer field while your daughter practices each day. It could include going bowling with friends, playing a round of golf on the weekends, or shooting hoops after work. Maybe jogging isn't your thing, but you've never branched out to see if a kickboxing class at the gym is your style.

My friend, Kip, has a beautiful, 75-year-old mom who has been taking ballroom dance lessons for years. She loves it. She is passionate about it and even competes every year in her age category. She has the body of someone half her age, and the high kicks!

Consider your workout personality. Do you prefer to work out alone and on your own time schedule? If so, then walking, cycling, running, weightlifting could be for you. If you like a workout partner or team companionship, then classes or team sports might be a good fit.

One of the biggest reasons people quit the exercise habit is lack of interest. If what you're doing isn't enjoyable and you dread it more than you desire it, it'll become a chore that's hard to maintain. Don't get me wrong. I am not saying that every morning I love getting up before the crows and sweating as I repeat one more rep of leg curls. However, afterwards, I always love how it makes me look and feel.

Bottom line: I stopped asking myself if I *feel* like going. I don't feel like brushing my teeth some mornings, but that doesn't mean I skip it.

3. Determine when you will work out.

Is there a better time of day to work out? Is 6 a.m. better than 6 p.m. in terms of being more efficient and leading you to a successful life? The truth is that there's no reliable evidence suggesting that only the early risers are more successful than the late nighters.

Yes, the title of this book is about completing your five disciplines before 8 o'clock in the morning, but I realize that not everyone is an early bird like me. Some of you are night owls and that's perfectly fine. It's about making exercise a regular, consistent part of your life, not what time of day you do it. There are pros and cons to each time of day. But your body has a rhythm; you have to discover it and adjust your schedule to flow with your preferred energy cycles.

Pros to a morning workout:
- You get it over with first thing in the morning.
- You have a boost of energy at the start of the day.
- You already feel productive, and it's not even seven o'clock.
- You kick start your metabolism early.
- You have more restful sleep.
- You tend to be more consistent.
- You have the most control over your day first thing in the morning.
- You're typically not expected to be anywhere at 5 or 6 a.m. other than in your bed, so you can protect this habit by doing it in the morning before anyone can interrupt your schedule.

Pros to a late afternoon/evening workout:
- You're already energetic for the day. My husband would never get up at the same hour as me. He's typically still sound asleep by the time I complete my five habits and I'm ready to run out the door for work. However, he is wide awake and full of energy in the evening when my body is winding down and my eyes are rolling back in my head.
- You can relieve stress from a long day.
- You could work out harder.
- Your sleep is improved. Yeah, I know I said the same thing with the morning workout, but the truth is that no matter what time of day you work out, exercise improves the quality of your rest.

There's no best time to work out, just the time that's best for you. Any time is a good time to exercise. Find what works best for your energy, your schedule, and your ability to be consistent.

4. Start Small.

This is so important in keeping you motivated. Most of the time, when we decide to start a new habit it's due to motivation. However, motivation doesn't last. It fluctuates based on how we feel. Remember, the goal of this book is not to get you inspired to change a few things that last three months. The point is to get you in the habit of doing things that eventually become second nature to you. If you're going to make this a part of your lifestyle, you need to begin with a realistic plan.

I always tell people, "Stop looking at the one hour you don't have and use the 20 minutes you do have." Over the years, I've received so many testimonies from people who started (and stuck with) a realistic 20-minute workout and lost significant amounts of weight. One lady started riding her stationary bike for 20 minutes a day while watching her favorite show and lost 30 pounds with a simple plan each day.

Begin with small changes in your diet. Replace one sugary drink (like my sweet tea) with one bottle of water each day. Start with an apple a day if you're used to no fruit in your diet. Add one salad to your meal if you never eat any greens. Fitness expert Chalene Johnson says, "Most diet books provide a variety of food, so you don't get bored. However, most fit people have only a handful of healthy spreads that are their go-to meals. They find something healthy they love and look forward to, and they stick to it." Johnson says, "*Have* a diet instead of going *on* a diet."[94] It is so important that you stick to the small changes, before you demand anything more radical from yourself. Remember, you want something that you can maintain your whole life not just torture yourself with massive changes for two months.

5. Make positive declarations over your body.

> **"The tongue of the wise promotes health."**
> **- Proverbs 12:18, NKJV**

Does your mouth have anything to do with your body size? Of course. But most people focus more on what's going in their mouths without any regard to what's coming out of their mouths when it pertains to weight loss and physical health. In my book, *Pep Talk*, I shared in detail the vital importance of making positive declarations over your body as it pertains to reaching your fitness goals.

In fact, I heard one medical doctor say that telling yourself, "I'll never lose weight" does as much damage as eating a whole bag of chips. As you're reading this book, you might even be saying, "Positive declarations don't work for weight loss" which is a declaration in itself. Consequently, it is working in your life. What if you put as much focused attention on what's coming *out* of your mouth as what's going *in* your mouth in order to reach your fitness goals? I believe you'd reach your ideal weight much quicker. I know I did.

Your words create your reality! If you want to reach your fitness goals and enjoy your life, then become extremely disciplined in what you speak over your body. According to behavioral psychologists, as much as 77% of your self-talk is negative or working against you, and it takes as many as 20 positive statements about yourself to counteract one negative personal declaration.[95]

The instant you find yourself affirming negative statements and behaviors about yourself, STOP! Instead of using your words to describe how you feel, use your words to change how you feel. Let your words be what they were designed to be: a tool to help you reach your goals. Plain and simple, your words control your life, your outcome, your results, even your physical well-being. Don't get me wrong, you may still think it, but don't speak it!

MY PERSONAL FITNESS AND HEALTH DECLARATIONS

For a complete list of my fitness declarations and my personal story of using declarations to get in shape, get a copy of my book, Pep Talk. Meanwhile, here are just a few of my personal declarations that I speak over my fitness and health habit.

I declare in the name of Jesus:

I am strong.

I am healthy.

I am in the best shape of my life.

I am beautiful inside and out.

I am free in my relationship with food.

I am fit, firm and muscular.

I feel good in my clothes.

I am happy with my body.

I have a fast metabolism.

I eat whatever I want to eat, and I maintain my perfect weight.

I am at my ideal weight.

I am full of energy.

I am dedicated to improving my health and fitness.

I am disciplined with exercise.

I look forward to working out.

I am confident in my appearance.

I am lean.

I am radiant and youthful.

I am secure in who I am and how I look.

I am an excellent example of godly confidence.

My Personalized Fitness Scriptures:

God has not given me a spirit of fear and timidity, but of power, love and self-discipline (2 Timothy 1:7, NLT).

I can do all things through Christ who strengthens me (Philippians 4:13, NKJV).

I prosper and live in good health even as my soul prospers (3 John 1:2, KJV).

I do everything to the glory of God, even my eating and drinking (1 Corinthians 10:31, NKJV).

My body is the home of the Holy Spirit, and He lives within me. It is a gift from God. He bought me with a great price, so I use my body to honor God (1 Corinthians 6:19–20, TLB).

I am energetic and strong, a hard worker (Proverbs 31:17 NLT).

No discipline is enjoyable while it is happening—it's painful! But afterward there will be a peaceful harvest of right living for me when I train myself this way. So I take a new grip with my hands and strengthen my knees. I mark out a straight path for my feet so that I will not fall but become strong (Hebrews 12:11–13, NLT).

6. Don't skip a day.

In the beginning of starting this new habit (or any new habit), don't miss a day. Even if it's only a 10-minute exercise session, do something. In Chapter 10, I'll explain the importance of seeing your progress on a habits calendar. This is vitally important in keeping yourself inspired and feeling competent.

I heard a professional fitness trainer say, "If I could summarize everything I've learned in 10 years of strength training, it would come down to these three words: Don't miss workouts." This is especially true when you're getting started with a new workout routine. We're prone to quit for extended periods of time when we "break the chain" of not staying committed for at least 21 days. If you can stick to something for at least 21-30 days, chances are you'll get into a routine that will become your lifestyle. Don't think about it as something you have to do for three to four weeks. Take it one day at a time.

Every single day counts. Don't skip any days while forming your habit.

But don't get discouraged if you mess up. Don't condemn yourself and stop the habit altogether if you skip a day. I want you to understand, this is a lifestyle change. It's about being in it long term, so don't give up what you want ultimately because of one slip-up.

When I started out my daily habits, I had to be rigid with my routine. My life had been in complete chaos so I had to give myself strict structure to change the course of my life. I had to wake up at the exact same time and do my habits in the exact same way each day, because I was overhauling my life. I was so desperate for change that I couldn't miss a single day. Rain or shine, I was out walking at the crack of dawn. The coldest day I remember going for a walk, the temperature was 15 below and I had to layer up with Rodney's jackets and gloves. I can't imagine what anyone who saw me must have thought!

But now that I've been doing these habits for nearly two decades, it's a way of life for me. I don't have to be quite so rigid now. I can give myself some leniency, because I know it's my way of life.

So when I say don't skip any days, it won't be that way for the rest of your life. You can give yourself leniency once it has become your lifestyle. But in the process of forming these habits, stay rigid. Stay consistence. No matter what. Stick to it! You can do anything for 30 days.

When you look back one month from now, you will be amazed and proud of this journey you began thirty days ago.

Extra tip: Always prepare the night before. Lay out your clothes, tennis shoes, food, water bottle, gym bag, etc. Lay everything out so there are no excuses or delays in getting you out the door ASAP. Preparation time is never wasted time!

MY DAILY ROUTINE

Sandi Castro Migliaccio
CEO of Safe Passage Pictures
Daily 5:

1. I start my day off with gratitude. As soon as I open my eyes I say thank you to God. I then pray and thank God for everything in my life, from the smallest of things to the big things.

2. Exercise daily. I'm on the treadmill in the morning for an hour and I end my day with running in Central Park.

3. I read 20 minutes from either success, inspirational, or motivational books.

4. I also read my Bible, read a daily devotional and write in my journal, even if it's 5 or 10 minutes.

5. Review my business goals and personal goals.

8

10 THINGS UNSUCCESSFUL PEOPLE DO

"Good habits are hard to form but easy to live with. Bad habits are easy to form but hard to live with."

Spotting a successful person with ambition, goals, determination, and a highly motivated, charismatic personality can be easy. But what about the ones who are habitually unsuccessful? Can you spot them as easily? I think you can. You have to wonder, are they practicing certain habits that are leading them to fail? And if they changed their habits, could it change their results? Absolutely.

The first successful man Darius Foroux ever met told him, "I just try to avoid being unsuccessful." The entrepreneur told Foroux to study what makes someone "unsuccessful, unhappy, broke, fat, stupid," in order to eliminate those things from your own life. "To this day," Darius said, "I still live by that advice. I like his concept of trying not to be unsuccessful."[96]

Now that we have identified the daily habits of the most successful people in the world, let's take a look at some of the bad habits the unsuccessful demonstrate.

Nobody is perfect and even highly successful people fall prey to some negative habits now and then, but the truth is there are certain consistent behaviors that could be stopping your success. The first step is to recognize those bad habits. In this chapter, I have outlined 10 of the habits of unsuccessful people, so that you know what to avoid as you make an all-out effort to achieve your goals and live your dreams. If you closely identify with any of the following 10 habits, then it's time to reevaluate your routines.

I admit, there are times when I have indulged in some of these negative actions, but let's strive to steer clear of them when we find ourselves falling into these detours that derail our dreams.

This may sound like an oxymoron, but I encourage you to be gentle, but firm (gently firm) on yourself as you go down the list of bad habits to see which ones you may identify with. Don't get discouraged; get determined. This entire book has proven that you can reinvent your life by making a few small changes in your daily routine.

MY DAILY ROUTINE

Dave Martin
President of Dave Martin International
Daily 5:

1. Order my day – set my daily schedule to maximize my time and effectiveness.

2. Spend time in the Bible – some days more than others, but each day some time.

3. Encourage someone and talk to someone who encourages me.

4. Give away something every day – maybe a coffee, maybe a kind word, maybe more...but this keeps me mindful of generosity.

5. Do something every day that moves me toward my goals – it may be a project, a phone call, research, a conference, or anything that propels me forward.

1. They complain.

> **"Instead of complaining that the rosebush is full of thorns, be happy that the thornbush has roses."**
> **- German Proverb**

People can identify exactly how successful or unsuccessful you are the moment you open your mouth. Ouch! I know, I don't like that either. The truth is, the only thing complaining does is convince other people that you are not in control. Complaining is a subconscious way of expressing that you are powerless to change your circumstances. When you complain about your debt, you are voicing hopelessness to be financially free. When you complain about your body, you are decreeing impossibilities to be in shape. When you complain about your job, you are expressing despair that it could never improve.

> **"Don't complain about something you don't have a vision to change."**
> **- Joyce Meyer**

If you're not going to make changes in your finances, to your body or place of employment, then don't complain about it. You chose it, you spent it, you ate it, you settled there. So don't complain about it. I know, that was a little more on the firm side than the gentle one.

Pay attention to how many things you complain about on a given day. You'll be surprised by how often a complaint comes out of your mouth. The traffic, the weather, how you slept, your hunger, your hair, the stoplight, your parking space, how crowded the restaurant is, the food is cold, your head hurts, your long list of to-do's, and how tired you are. The list is endless. And we do it without even noticing we're doing it.

Here's the result. When you complain about your life, the only thing you'll get is a lot more to complain about. You get what you focus on. Remember that road trip game "Slug Bug" that kids would play in the car so that they could yell "Slug Bug" and punch each other every time they saw a VW Bug on the road? As soon as they start looking for Volkswagen Beetles, kids will find them all over the place. Complaining works the same way. It magnifies the negatives in your life so much that it crowds out the potential for you to see anything else.

Complaining has internal and external consequences. It drains your energy and causes you to subconsciously feel hopeless about your circumstances. Your self-esteem takes a hit when you believe you can't change anything in your life. It's also contagious. When you complain, it spreads to those around you and brings your entire atmosphere down.

With these results, I'm sure you can see how nothing delays your progress more than complaining. When you complain, you remain! Jim Rohn said, "Indulge in this slightly and you might as well forget the future. If you spend five minutes complaining, you have just wasted five minutes. If you continue complaining, it won't be long before they haul you out to a financial desert and there let you choke on the dust of your own regret." He was a little dramatic! But it's true. Complaining is an utter waste of time, and it can ruin you.

Consider the story of the Israelites headed to the Promised Land, the land of abundance, when their trip was delayed by 40 years. Why? Because they obsessively complained. They griped about the water, the weather, the food, the leadership, the distance, the climate, the desert, the people. Here's the shocking news: Their trip should have taken 11 days, but it took them four decades!

What circumstances are you circling year after year, making little progress, due to your enormous amount of complaints? Is it the mountain of weight loss you keep going around? Rather than focus on your progress, you've magnified the lack of results? Complain and you'll remain.

Could it be the mountain of marital problems? Rather than pinpoint the good in your spouse, you zero in on the bad and magnify it to such a degree that it crowds out any potential for restoration? Complain and you'll remain.

Could it be the mountain of financial problems? Rather than focus on paying off one debt, you get overwhelmed at the pile of bills and the empty savings account, so you gripe about the home, car and utilities that you used to see as blessings. Complain and you'll remain.

> ## "The more you complain about your problems, the more problems you'll have to complain about."
> ## - Zig Ziglar

David Horsager, author of *The Trust Factor*, said, "Eighteen years ago, my mentor asked me to make a ninety-day commitment to stop complaining." Horsager said, "It absolutely changed my life!"[97] He's now a bestselling author featured in *Fast Company, Forbes, Wall Street Journal,* and his clients include companies such as Wells Fargo, Goodyear, Dept. of Homeland Security, and the New York Yankees! It all began by making a commitment to stop complaining.

Philippians 2:14 says, "Do *all things* without grumbling and fault-finding and complaining…" (AMPC, emphasis added). That's a pretty clear command. No complaints!

Remember that every word you speak has some kind of outcome on your life. Are your words taking you closer to or further from your goals? Proverbs 18:21 says that our words have the power of life or death in them. What you say matters! Avoid complaining at all cost.

Think of it this way, on your road to success, what do you want people to hear when you open your mouth? Complaints or gratitude? When you complain, you sound powerless. When you're grateful, you sound powerful. I love this quote, "If we want to complain, there will always be things to complain about. If we want to be grateful, there will always be things to be grateful about. The beauty is that the choice is up to us."[98]

2. They are always late.

Are you the friend who shows up to the wedding after the bride has already made it to the altar? You try to tiptoe in the ceremony hoping you haven't drawn away much attention from the vows and whisper your apologies to the *prompt* guests who quietly scoot over to make space for you?

Are you the patient who arrives 15 minutes late for the dentist appointment leaving the receptionist in a bind trying to move other appointments around? Or the family member everyone is waiting on while the food is getting cold?

"What late people don't understand about on-time people," comedian Mike Birbiglia says in a stand-up routine, "is that we hate them. Getting a reputation as a latie is not a good thing!"[99]

For some people, being on time seems almost impossible. Even if they have all day to prepare for an evening dinner out, they are still running around in a frenzy trying to get out the door 10 minutes late.

I was at a restaurant the other day with a group of ladies and one of them arrived about 15 minutes late. Laughing it off (as no indicator of being unsuccessful), she said, "I'm late to everything. It's the story of my life." To be honest, it's no laughing matter.

Chronic lateness communicates a subtle, yet strong, message: You're inconsiderate of other people's schedules, you're a procrastinator, you're not an effective time manager, you're selfish, you are unreliable, and you're not in control. Wow! I feel bad even typing those descriptions. However, study after study shows this to be the message you're unintentionally giving through your lateness.

I don't want to be too harsh in this chapter, so please don't get me wrong. I'm not saying that you should never be late and if you are, you're a loser. Even with the best intentions and scheduling ahead, it's impossible to not be late sometimes. It's happened to me. I get the unplanned phone call, the train crossing that I didn't factor in, the hair that refuses to style right, and the eyelash that won't stay on!

However, it turns into a roadblock to success when people anticipate your lateness with pristine accuracy. When you're always late to everything: church, dinners, sporting events, family gatherings, doctor appointments, weddings, funerals, airport pick-ups, and work, that's when it's a major problem, and it reflects your integrity (or lack of it).

I've spoken many times for Harvest Church in London, where they pay strict attention to starting their weekly services on time. Pastor Jo Naughton previously held a prestigious job in marketing for the Prince of Wales before she and her husband, Paul, began pastoring. With her adorable British accent, she said, "I can't, for the life of me, understand how anyone would consider showing up late for church." She explained, "When I worked for the Prince, you arrived early and were in place eagerly awaiting his royal arrival. To be late would be inconceivable." Her next statement struck me deeply, "Lateness wasn't tolerated for the Prince, why should it be for the King of Kings?!" Point well taken.

In his article (and I love this title), "Being Late Says a Lot About You and None of It's Good," John West says that when you break a "time promise" it's not without consequence. He says, "Every time you do it, you are sending a subtle message to the person you stood up that they are less important than you or whatever you were doing. It also says that you aren't dependable, reliable, or maybe even honest. And let's face it, all that adds up to making you an icky person to work with."[100]

So, if you think punctuality doesn't matter, think again. When you make this small but significant change in your routine, it instantly communicates a strong message that you care, you're responsible, you're in control, you're proactive, and you have the habits of a successful person.

3. They blame others.

Unsuccessful people always point the finger at someone else for why they are where they are in life. Some call it a victim mentality. They will give you every reason in the book as to why they can't succeed: the government, the economy, the lack of education, the lack of time, poor parenting, the ex-spouse, the President, you name it. It's never their own fault.

Truthfully, this started all the way back in Genesis when Eve blamed the serpent and Adam blamed Eve for why they couldn't keep God's instruction to not eat the forbidden fruit. Nobody wanted to take responsibility for that life-altering consequence.

Blaming others solves nothing. We make choices, and our choices have consequences. When you learn to take personal responsibility for where you are in life, it's a massive step on the road to being successful.

In the first chapter of Jack Canfield's life-changing book, *The Success Principles*, he states that the first key to success is to take 100% responsibility for your life. There is only one person responsible for the outcome of your life and that's you.

When you take personal responsibility for your life rather than blame others for your outcome, you are admitting that your decisions have led to your current health, your debt, your relationships, your body, your lifestyle, your success or lack thereof. It's all because of you. That's hard to admit, but it's also a forward step in taking responsibility and turning your poor choices into successful ones.

As a young aspiring speaker, Zig Ziglar heard the statement, "You are where you are because that's exactly where you chose to be." Ziglar said, at the time he was "broke, in debt, and down in the dumps. It came through loud and clear that I was where I was and what I was because of the choices and decisions I made!"[101]

We like to look for a cause, a reason, or an excuse so we can let ourselves off the hook. People will blame the bad hand they were dealt in life, that life isn't fair, and they spend their energy feeling sorry for themselves. But that's all one big excuse for their own failure to succeed.

The truth is, that it takes a big person to accept and admit that they messed up, made bad choices, took the wrong turn, and ended up in a less than desirable place in life. When everything that goes wrong in your life is somebody else's fault, you're sending yourself the message that you are powerless, and you place yourself in the passenger's seat of your own destiny.

Are you truly that powerless? No! You have the choice today to get in the driver's seat by taking 100% responsibility for where you go from this day forward.

> **"For we are each responsible for**
> **our own conduct."**
> **- Galatians 6:5, NLT**

4. They waste money.

If money's always burning a hole in your pocket, you're setting yourself up for failure. Financially unsuccessful people—as I was for many years—have no idea where all their money is going. They aren't frugal with their finances, and they have a habit of making spontaneous purchases with no regard to the consequence of high interest payments or the foregoing of savings for the future. They tend to live in the moment.

This group of over-spenders lives beyond their means racking up credit card debt because they can't seem to delay gratification. If they want something, they get it…whether they can afford it or not. After all, they don't really know if they can afford it because they don't have a budget.

"Your money habits can make you rich or put you in the poor house," Tom Corley of *Rich Habits* boldly states. He cites a study done by Brown University when he says, "Most of the habits we pick up in life come from our parents. This includes money habits. If your parents had bad money habits, it is likely those habits rubbed off on you. But in order to change bad money habits, you need to first become aware of them."[102]

If your parents didn't place a high priority on saving and investing, you naturally won't either. Corley spent five years studying habits of the rich and the poor. He reports that, "Eighty-eight percent of the poor in my study had over $5,000 in revolving credit-card debt. Sixty-nine percent used those credit cards to purchase big-ticket items. And 77% had multiple credit cards." Corley went on to explain, "Sixty-one percent of the poor did not own their homes—they rented them—while 100% of the rich owned their homes. When you don't own your home, you are unable to build home equity."[103]

Other items the unsuccessful tend to waste money on are: fast food, gambling, playing the lottery, expensive electronic devices, new cars, renting furniture and appliances, late fees, vacations, etc.

There are so many shiny items vying for our attention, and retail therapy definitely makes us feel happy! A weekend getaway, a spa treatment, or an expensive cupcake does wonders to boost our spirits. But in the long run, spending money we don't have (in our bank, not on our credit cards) leads to the stress of living beyond our means.

The biggest drain on our money can be eating out. The lunch you didn't cook because you weren't in the mood adds up. If you spend $10 a day (multiplied by four days a week), it's costing you over $2,000 a year on that salad, the burrito, the muffin, and the sandwich you could have made before you ran out of the house. Imagine that two grand going in a savings account or towards your dream vacation. Instead, your financial future was (literally) eaten up by poor decisions.

Proverbs 29:18 is true in every area of our lives. Where there is no financial vision, your money will perish. However, when you have a financial target, a goal, a clear, compelling vision to save $1,000, to pay off a credit card, to go on a dream trip, to open an investment account (and secure your future), it's amazing how it guides every financial decision you make.

Unsuccessful people don't have financial goals; therefore, they spend and spend and spend. They spend more than they earn.

If you can't pay cash for what you want, don't get it. You can't afford it right now. Save up for it. Earn it. Enjoy the thrill of knowing you truly earned this thing.

5. They surround themselves with other unsuccessful people.

Remember when your mom came unglued because you started hanging out with the girl who could date way before you could or the guy who had a reputation for being a rebel? Well, adult friends have the same influence in derailing your success.

Nearly everyone knows that their closest friends can affect their life, but what most people don't realize is how profound this influence is on your level of success. They affect your self-confidence, your beliefs, your behaviors, your spending habits, your health choices, your religious and political views, your discipline or lack thereof and much more.

Do you want to get fit? Hang out with fit people. Do you want to be rich? Spend time with rich people. We tend to feed off each other's energy. If your friends typically swing through the drive-thru for lunch every day, you'll sit right beside them and join the ride. If your closest companions watch the latest reality TV shows, you'll swap stories on your coffee break. You become like those with whom you spend the most time.

In fact, an experiment was conducted between a monkey that never feared snakes and a monkey who was terror-stricken by them. They were placed in the same space together with the harmless reptile. The brave monkey began to show fear of the snakes when it saw the anxious response of the other monkey that was frightened. These little monkeys illustrate how behaviors, insecurities, and fears are contagious; but so is confidence and courage.[104]

How do you tend to behave when you're around your inner circle? Do your wildest impulses take over? Do you tend to drink too much alcohol, eat more junk food, talk negatively about other people, complain, or spend foolishly? If so, then these friends are not supporting your new mindset for success.

On the contrary, when you leave a dinner outing with your friends, do you jump in your car feeling inspired, stretched, encouraged, and challenged to come up higher? Then, you've got the right associations.

I'm not saying that you and your BFF don't have the occasional dump-it-all-out session where you vent everything that's bothering you. Like Dionne Warwick sang, "That's what friends are for." But that's not all they're intended to be. They should be supporters of your success habits and help to push you further along.

Jesus loved everyone. Tax collectors. Prostitutes. Thieves. Adulterers. Everyone. But He was selective about His inner circle. Yes, He had twelve men around Him, but He spent most of His ministry with only three: Peter, James, and John.

Successful people are careful and intentional about their inner circle. If you are the average of your five closest friends, look at the five people around you. What are their disciplines? What are their goals and aspirations for life? Do they support yours or derail yours?

"Walk with the wise and become wise, associate with fools and get in trouble."
- Proverbs 13:20, NLT

6. They watch a lot of TV.

Life is meant to be lived, not watched. Unsuccessful people waste valuable time watching others live their dreams rather than eliminate even an hour to go invest in their own. It's easy to do. We have an unbelievable amount of viewing options. Anything from documentaries to weather-by-the-minute, fashion design, dramas, home makeovers, reality shows, and an entire network dedicated to nothing but food 24-hours-a-day.

Watching television is as much a habit as brushing teeth. We come in from work, plop down on the sofa, and grab the remote. Four hours later, we get ready for bed, and some even turn the TV on again. It's perfectly fine to enjoy watching television occasionally. But to be successful, your time should be managed properly, not wasted on way too much meaningless entertainment.

We've already seen how startling it can be to discover how much time you could be wasting glued to a flat-screened rectangle in your living room. When you see the numbers in black-and-white, hopefully, it will compel you to start eliminating as much wasted time as possible.

Our televisions have become major focal points in American homes. Think about it. We decorate our houses around our TVs. We point our furniture at them. We put them in multiple rooms. Ninety-five percent of Americans watch TV daily, and the typical American views over five hours of TV every single day!

What does that mean? If we break those numbers down even more, it reveals that the average person is watching close to 1,700 hours of

TV each year! That's one thousand seven hundred hours of sitting on your bottom watching others fall in love, start businesses, travel the world, have families, and report gossip about people you don't even know! So, if the average lifespan is around 78 years old, that equates to about 15 years spent staring at a screen! Fifteen years of your life![105]

These are the idle habits that are being ingrained and adapted into our children. Nowadays, TV's can be found in nearly every room of the house, but we don't even need a TV because we have access to the shows on our smart phones and tablets. Television entertainment has become a pacifier for babies, a comforter for children, and entertainment for the family.

With cities providing parks, schools providing extracurricular activities, neighborhoods adding sidewalks, and American garages full of outdoor toys like scooters, skateboards, and bikes, our families have multitudes of entertainment that add value to our lives. Unfortunately, U.S. residents are still spending more time than any other country sitting still, watching show after show.

"If you add up all the time that the *average* American spends with electronic media (TV, computers, smart phones, radio, etc.) it's around 11 and a half hours per day," says entertainment journalist, Dustin Rowles.[106] Most of us can probably admit that we indulge in this non-productive habit more than we care to admit.

Thomas Corley, whose study of the wealthy and poor I quoted earlier wrote, "Seventy-eight percent of the poor watch reality TV shows. The rich, on the other hand, are not big on TV. Sixty-seven percent watch less than an hour each day and it's not reality TV that they tune in to."[107]

When I share these startling facts at conferences, I jokingly say, "If the average American is watching 5 hours of TV each day, and you eliminate 20 minutes to go read, listen to a podcast, or go for a walk, you will have invested 10 hours of progress over the course of a

month...and you can still watch your 4 hours and 40 minutes of TV!"
Imagine what you could do if you eliminated more than 20 minutes.

> **"Any successful entrepreneur knows**
> **that time is more valuable than**
> **money itself." - Richard Branson**

7. They don't take care of their health.

Sixty-eight percent of American adults are overweight or obese.[108] Tom
Corley found in his study that 76% of the wealthiest people exercise
at least four days a week, whereas, only 23% of the poor. Most highly
successful people realize the importance of taking care of themselves
physically. So why doesn't everyone consider this a priority?

Excuses.

Every single person has the same 24 hours in a day. Some find time
to exercise and some find excuses to not. What we habitually do each
day is either promoting health or destroying it. The choice is ours.

I grew up exercising by consistently being involved in sports.
Whether it was gymnastics, cheerleading, or track, I was always
moving. When I got married and started working a full-time job,
I was no longer walking three miles a day to college classes and my
days consisted of sitting at a desk for eight hours straight (with a
one-hour lunch break). The outcome was not what I anticipated.

I remember joining a gym with my best friend, and we enrolled
in a water aerobics class. We had so much fun every Tuesday and
Thursday night bouncing around the pool with a bunch of 60-year-old
women. However, as the weeks went by, after getting off work at 5:00
p.m., making a hot meal, sitting down in front of the TV and getting
comfortable, the thought of jumping into a cold swimming pool sent
chills all over my body. It was the last thing I wanted to do. So, the

Tuesday/Thursday plan went from some Tuesdays and no Thursdays to nothing. I was right there with the others full of excuses as to why I couldn't make it to class.

Thinking about their physical well-being is not a priority for unsuccessful people. They eat junk food, drink everything but water, and see exercise as something they'll get around to one day.

Here's a list of some excuses the unsuccessful make about their health:[109]

1. I don't have time.

    It's hard to justify this excuse when we've uncovered how much time the average American is wasting watching television each day. And that didn't include the time invested scrolling Facebook, filtering photos on Instagram, and retweeting your favorite celebrity, not to mention playing Candy Crush.

    I mean, if you have to watch at least four hours of your favorite dramas, at least grab a resistance band or jump on a mini-trampoline and utilize that time to exercise. Some activity is always better than none.

    Rather than search for excuses, find solutions: Take the stairs instead of the elevator. Park the farthest from the grocery store. Walk during your lunch break or around the soccer field while your kids practice. We find time for things we value in our lives. When we start to value our health, we'll value our time to invest in it.

2. I'm too tired. Remember, the funny thing is that working out actually gives you more energy. Your body produces hormones (endorphins) that produce energy when you exercise. In fact, Isaac Newton's first law of motion is often stated as: "An object at rest stays at rest and an object in motion stays in motion." This is not just about physics; it's about your physical health as well.

3. It's too expensive. You don't have to join the pricey health club or trendy cycling class to care about your health. You can simply walk around your neighborhood, go bowling, circle the floors at the shopping mall, play a game of laser tag, walk the dog, or ride bikes with your kids.

4. I'm not motivated. When you don't have a vision for your physical body, you'll lack the drive to stick with an exercise habit. Once you get a vision for how you want to look and the action steps to get there, you'll develop the habits that lead you to your dreams. You'll enjoy the positive comments from others and overall feel good about yourself for sticking with it.

8. They gossip.

Are you so busy talking about other people's lives that you miss out on your own? What about your unique goals, dreams, and aspirations? Don't forget who you are and what you should be doing instead of worrying about what everyone else is doing.

> **"Gossiping is like throwing a boomerang—what you toss out, comes back to you."**

Galatians 6:7 says, "Do not be deceived: God cannot be mocked. A man reaps what he sows" (NIV). From this scripture, we can see that when you talk badly about other people, you are *sowing seed*, so-to-speak, for others to talk badly about you. When you put people down, you're *sowing seed* for others to put you down. When you make fun of someone, you are *sowing seed* for others to make fun of you!

Haven't you heard that when you point a finger at someone else, there are three fingers pointed back at you? Well, it's scientific. In fact,

179

research has found that when you talk negatively to a friend about how terrible another friend, colleague, or relative is, the listening friend is more likely to associate the negativity to *you* rather than to the person you're describing. Behavioral psychologists call this "spontaneous trait transference." In other words, your subtle intentions of making someone else look bad backfires on you.

I love this quote from Eleanor Roosevelt as a way of identifying where people are at in their mindset and journey to success (and to even check up on myself from time-to-time): "Big minds talk about ideas. Average minds talk about events. Small minds talk about people."

When you get around someone who constantly talks badly about people, puts them down, makes fun of them, and tries to make them look bad, they just gave you a strong look into their limited mindset.

The truth is that it's so easy to get caught up in gossip. French social psychologist, Laurent Bègue found that "about 60% of conversations between adults are about someone who isn't present," he says. "And most of these are passing judgment."[110]

Some people get emotional satisfaction from talking about how awful other people are. Some are so bored with their own lives that they have nothing else to focus on than to critique, judge, and belittle someone who's doing something significant with their life.

One article I read put it this way, "Unsuccessful people are often unhappy as a result of refusing to take responsibility for their lack of effort and achievement. They compensate by trying to pull down the achievements of others. It all stems from their jealousy of those who put in the work, take smart risks, and achieve more success in their lives. It's an exhausting way to live, and it rarely leads to anything good."[111]

I like the Pinterest graphic that says, "I'm too busy watering my own grass to notice if yours is greener." That's the attitude of a successful person. They're not watching everyone else, competing with their success, or feeling insecure. No, they stay in their lane, focused on their unique vision without concerning themselves with what others are doing. God is going to hold you accountable for what He's called *you* to do, not what He's called others to do.

God's Word reveals a chilling reality of gossip in Numbers 12:1, "Then Miriam and Aaron spoke *against* Moses...." The next verse says, "...And the Lord heard it" (Numbers 12:2). Wow! God hears us when we honor people, and He also hears us when we dishonor people. Doesn't that make you think twice about what you say?

Remember, if you don't approve of something someone is doing or you get in a discussion where others are gossiping, God is listening. And He's not favorable toward it.

If you're not experiencing a lot of favor, opportunities or growth in your life, take an inventory of what's been coming out of your mouth. How have you been speaking about people? Are you trying to make others look bad so you can appear better? Are you intimidated by their success so you try to dim the light on them so yours can shine brighter? It's not working. You can't talk badly about people and not expect people to talk badly about you. It's the law of the boomerang.

The good news is the opposite is true as well. When you talk well of others, you are sowing seed for others to talk well of you. I like the *Phillips* translation of Galatians 6:7, "Don't be under any illusion: you cannot make a fool of God! A man's harvest in life will depend entirely on what he sows."

"Silence can never be misquoted."

9. They procrastinate.

"Tomorrow is the only day of the year that appeals to a lazy man."
- Jimmy Lyons

So far, we have outlined eight bad habits of the unsuccessful, but the biggest guarantee for a life of missed opportunities is through procrastination. *Procrastination* is defined as "the act of putting off, delaying or deferring an action to a later time; to put off intentionally or habitually." Procrastinators sabotage their own success.

"There is a tremendous cost in putting things off," said Steve Pavlina, "You don't get paid for your thoughts and plans—you only get paid for your results."[112]

Psychology Today reported that 20% of people identify themselves as chronic procrastinators. "For them procrastination is a lifestyle," the author writes. "And it cuts across all domains of their life. They don't pay bills on time. They miss opportunities for buying tickets to concerts. They don't cash gift certificates or checks. They file income tax returns late. They leave their Christmas shopping until Christmas Eve."[113]

We all procrastinate, to a degree, on certain matters. We sit down to work on an important project and next thing you know we're scrolling through Instagram, loading the dishwasher, eating a snack, and googling what our childhood celebrity crush looks like nowadays. Suddenly, the day is gone, and we've put the project off another 24 hours.

The difference is habitual procrastinators give in to the distraction of instant gratification from doing any task that requires great effort.

Procrastinators live by the "I'll do it tomorrow" mentality.

- I'll start the diet tomorrow.
- I'll return the phone call tomorrow.
- I'll get the oil changed tomorrow.
- I'll finish the report tomorrow.
- I'll start waking up earlier tomorrow.
- I'll start saving money, working out, reading more, spending time with God...tomorrow.

Second Corinthians 6:1 says, "…we beg you, please don't squander one bit of this marvelous life God has given us" (MSG). That's exactly what procrastination does: It squanders minutes and hours and days from this limited time we have on earth.

The Washington Post reported on an experiment conducted to help procrastinators make better decisions. They found that when chronic procrastinators were told to focus on their future selves rather than their current condition, they followed through with swift decisions. They even went as far as to digitally age the participants by using current photographs of themselves. "Those who were more in touch with their future selves—both two months and 10 years down the line—reported fewer procrastination behaviors."[114]

I love what Pope Paul VI said, "Somebody should tell us, right at the start of our lives, that we are dying. Then we might live life to the limit, every minute of every day. Do it, I say! Whatever you want to do, do it now! There are only so many tomorrows."

W. Clement Stone, who built an insurance empire worth hundreds of millions of dollars, used to hand out lapel pins for all his employees that read, "Do it now!" In addition, he would make them all recite it at the start of each workday. He was convinced that this chant would reprogram their thinking and stop delays in their tracks. And he was right.

When you get inspired to do something, to change a habit, to set a new goal, to establish a new routine, make the change within twenty-four hours, or chances are, you never will.

"He slept beneath the moon; He basked beneath the sun. He lived a life of going-to-do; And died with nothing done.
- James Alberty

10. They quit.

Unsuccessful people have a pattern of quitting. They quit the diet when the dessert tray is brought out. They quit the debt-freedom plan when the shoe sale is too good of a deal. They quit the early-rise commitment when they hear the sound of rain outside. They quit the semester when the exams are too stressful. They just quit.

A quitter is defined as "a person who gives up easily or does not have the courage or determination to finish a task." Statistics show that 80% of Americans who set New Year's goals each year quit by February.[115] Nearly 25% don't even last a full seven days! Forty-two percent admit to never succeeding and fail on their resolution each year. Only 8% of people achieve their New Year's resolutions.[116]

Most of us have quit something we wish we hadn't, but when this becomes our typical response in hard times, that's when failure is inevitable. We will encounter delays, detours, and even discouragement on the road to success, but that's part of the process. Obstacles are the very things that strengthen us to handle success when it comes.

There is a story of bumblebees being taken into space. These winged creatures floated through the air with such ease, no exertion required. The bumblebees adapted to a life of simplicity. However, on the fourth day, the bumblebees all died. It was concluded that the bees were not designed to live without any resistance. And neither were we. Resistance prepares you, strengthens you, and enables you to go to the next level.

Here are some of the excuses you'll hear quitters make:

1. **It wasn't their goal to begin with.**

   Have you ever set a goal that you didn't truly care about? Did someone else influence you to set this goal but you never truly took ownership of it? It could be a spouse implying you should spend less, co-worker convincing you to try a new gluten-free diet, or a parent hoping for you to complete your college degree. When it's not something you have bought into, then it's difficult to stay motivated when the going gets tough.

2. **It's taking too long.**

    When we don't see results quick enough, it's tempting to quit altogether. Every successful person knows that achievement takes time. It's not that you're not doing the right thing, you're just not doing it long enough to see results. That's exactly why this book is about changing your habits and your routine.

3. **It's too hard.**

    When reaching a goal is more grueling than we anticipated, it can be demotivating. When others reached their goal in half the time it's taking you, it can be quite convincing to throw in the towel. But the thing that's tempting you to give up will become what you're most proud of because you didn't give in.

No one's life is without struggles. Many times it feels like you're taking three steps forward and two steps back, but you're still a step ahead. The key is to teach yourself to focus on the positives. You are making progress. It all adds up over time. Focus on progress not perfection.

Be Encouraged

This chapter lists 10 bad habits we should do our best to steer clear of, but don't let it be a discouragement. Don't be overwhelmed with tackling so many life changes all at once or you'll fall into the temptation to quit. Habits that took you years to build won't change in a few days. This book is designed to provide awareness to subconscious patterns that could be the anchor pulling you down when God is ready to lift you higher.

MY DAILY ROUTINE

Paula White-Caine
Founder of Paula White Ministries
Daily 5:

1. Read the Word, pray and journal.

2. Spend time with my husband. We usually have coffee, enjoy conversation and our morning together!

3. Exercise or ride my horse.

4. Set my to-do list for the day.

5. Read a book or something I am studying or tackle my most priority emails.

9

THE SECRET TO SELF-MOTIVATION

Motivation makes things happen. Where there's no will, there's no way. Self-motivation is the key to success. Most people have at least some desire to achieve an elevated level of success no matter where they are in life. It could be to live in a nicer house, to drive a better car, to be promoted in the company, to earn a larger salary, to have a more enjoyable marriage, experience a more lavish lifestyle, or leave a lasting legacy for their family. Without a clear vision of success (for you), you won't be able to pinpoint your destination. And if you don't know where you're headed, how will you know when you arrive?

Proverbs 29:18 says, "Where there is no vision, the people perish." Other translations say the people throw off restraint, self-control, or self-discipline. The late Myles Munroe put it this way, "The key to your future is finding a vision that imposes self-discipline on you."[117] Discipline comes from having a clear, compelling vision of what success means to you. Vision simplifies life, controls your choices, and shows you your destination. When your vision is clear, if something doesn't line up with your idea of success, it's easier to resist.

You can't live the life of your dreams if you never dream of it.

Likewise, you can't live a successful life if you never define what success means to you. You see, success is a personal thing. What motivates one person may be radically different for someone else. Until you define what living a successful life means to you, you'll struggle with staying inspired to fulfill your daily habits.

Merriam-Webster defines success as "the fact of getting or achieving wealth, respect, or fame," but this interpretation doesn't totally describe it for me. Throughout this book, I referred to the habits of successful people. In most cases, if not all, the reference of success typically meant someone who's earned millions if not billions of dollars, authored bestselling books, run large companies or even nations, and basically, lives a rock star lifestyle. However, if you ask these individuals their definitions for success, many will admit that the stuff they have accumulated and the achievements they have attained aren't what make them feel accomplished.

Look at some of the definitions for success from some well-known, *successful* people:

- Coach John Wooden, the winningest coach in college basketball history: "Success is peace of mind, which is a direct result of self-satisfaction in knowing you did your best to become the best you are capable of becoming."
- Acclaimed author Maya Angelou: "Success is liking yourself, liking what you do, and liking how you do it."
- Spiritual teacher Deepak Chopra: "No. 1, the progressive realization of worthy goals. No. 2, the ability to love and have compassion. No. 3, to be in touch with the creative source inside you. And no. 4, to ultimately move from success to significance."
- Billionaire Sir Richard Branson: "The more you're actively and practically engaged, the more successful you will feel."
- Prime Minister Winston Churchill: "Success is going from failure to failure without losing enthusiasm."
- Inventor Thomas Edison: "Success is 1% inspiration, 99%

perspiration."

- Bill Gates: "It is also nice to feel like you made a difference—inventing something or raising kids or helping people in need."
- John Paul DeJoria, co-founder of John Paul Mitchell: "Success isn't how much money you have. Success is not what your position is. Success is how well you do what you do when nobody else is looking."[118]

In Zig Ziglar's last book, *Born to Win! Find Your Success Code*, he shares his definitions for success:

What Success Is:

1. Success is knowing that you did a great job when you close the door to your office at the end of each workday and head for home.
2. Success is having a home and people to love who love you in return.
3. Success is having the financial security to meet your obligations each month and the knowledge that you have provided that security for your family in the event of your demise.
4. Success is having the kind of faith that lets you know where to turn when there seems to be no place to turn.
5. Success is having an interest or hobby that gives you joy and peace.
6. Success is knowing who you are, and Whose you are.
7. Success is taking good care of you and waking up healthy each day.
8. Success is slipping under the covers at the end of the day and realizing with gratitude that, "It just doesn't get much better than this!"[119]

MY DAILY ROUTINE

Dr. Caroline Leaf
Cognitive neuroscientist, author
Daily 5:

1. Controlling my thought life: I spend around 7-16 minutes every morning gathering and reflecting on my thoughts, seeing what I need to change in my life and focusing on what I am thankful for. I use the 21 day detox process I developed in my clinical research.

2. I spend around 2 hours a day doing research—intellectual stimulation is essential when it comes to our mental health.

3. I start the day off with organic, fair trade black coffee, a good healthy organic breakfast and I make sure every meal I eat is sustainably grown, farmed, and prepared.

4. Every morning and evening I follow a specific skin care routine using organic products and spending between 30 minutes to 1 hour in my infrared sauna.

5. I make sure that I spend daily time talking to and laughing with those I love, my husband and children, and building a strong support system that is there for all of us when we are going through tough times.

You can see from this list that success is defined many different ways, unique to each person.

The secret to self-motivation begins with finding *your* definition of success. It will be the fuel to get you up in the morning and the drive that keeps you awake at night. You must have a reason to succeed. Why is it so important to you? What will you lose if you don't keep going? I want to help you answer these questions in a way that ignites your desire to become disciplined and self-motivated.

Let me show you how I discovered my own definition for success and how it's kept me motivated all these years.

1. Define a successful life for you.

Mark Twain said, "The two greatest days in a person's life are the day you were born and the day you discover why." I believe once you define success on your terms, it gives you a clear picture of where you need to direct your attention and the steps you need to take to get there.

I like to explain this process as if you were handed a bag of 10,000 little puzzle pieces without the picture on the box. You have no idea what these little cardboard chips are supposed to create. Is it the Eiffel Tower? A cupcake with buttercream icing? A field full of daisies? What is this bag of nonsense? However, your job each day is to get up, go to the kitchen table and try to figure this puzzle out. Day after day, you have no idea what you're creating, but you keep working tirelessly to discover the mysterious image. Over time, you would get frustrated, bored, irritated, and lethargic. Why? Because you don't even know what you're doing. Ahhh, but once someone hands you the picture, it all starts to come together. You put the photo in sight and begin finding the pieces to match the image in front of you.

That's what happens when you define success for your life. You develop an image of what your life should look like when you come to the end. You imagine your great-grandkids describing your legacy, your values, your heritage. In fact, Stephen Covey, author of the bestselling book, *The 7 Habits of Highly Effective People,* defined success in a way that I personally connect with: "If you carefully consider what you want to be said of you in the funeral experience, you will find your definition of success."[120]

The Assignment of a Lifetime

Let me share with you a personal story that I shared in my first book, *Make Your Dreams Bigger than Your Memories,* of how this unusual act impacted my life for more than three decades and helped me pinpoint my definition of success.

"Class, I want you to get out a sheet of paper and write your full name at the top," said my high school English teacher, Mrs. Sawyer. "Underneath your name, write your birthdate, and last night's date." We all obeyed the instructions; however, we were totally unclear as to what this assignment had to do with diagraming sentences and reporting on current events. Then, she gave this chilling directive, "Now, I want each of you to write your own obituary."

What? I thought, as the entire class of young, healthy, 17-year-olds looked around at each other completely confused and a little creeped out by this morbid assignment.

"What would people say about you at your funeral?" Mrs. Sawyer bluntly asked. "Give it some thought," she said. "What would your parents say about you? How would your siblings describe you? How would your closest friends describe your personality? How did you spend your time? What were you known for? Who did you help? What would your pastor say about you?"

After she got our minds thinking about all these compelling questions in a way we had never done before, she added this twist, "Class, before you start, I don't want you to write what you've done up to this time in your life. I don't want you to write how your friends and family would currently describe you. I want you to write what you *want* to be said about you at your funeral someday."

You see, this awkward and startling assignment was the result of one of the high school students, who was my friend, losing his life the night before. There was a great sense of loss and sadness in the atmosphere on the school grounds. We were at a loss for words and still in shock at his sudden, accidental death less than 12 hours prior. Her directive had us on the edge of our seats. If a 17-year-old classmate could lose his life in a tragic, freak accident, what made us any different? What if that had been me who fell out of a truck, by accident, and was run over in front of the school grounds? What stories would people be sharing about me this Friday morning?

My deceased friend, Paul, didn't get another day, month or even year to make any more decisions with his life. He only had the short 17 years he was given on earth to live it the best way possible, and I'm glad to say, he did.

This assignment was more than thought-provoking; it was life-changing, destiny-pointing, and discipline-provoking. More than thirty years later, I obviously still think about Mrs. Sawyer's English class that September morning in 1985. As we completed our assignment that day, Mrs. Sawyer held out her hand to collect the obituaries and made this statement, "Students, you have not only written your obituaries, you've written your dreams...now, go live them."

Wow! What a profound and life-altering assignment. But it's not for high school students alone; it's for you. It's for anyone and everyone who wants to live a life designed to succeed on purpose. It's for anyone who longs to make the years matter and the days count. It's for you today to trigger self-motivation like never before.

When you come to the end of your life and you look back, what do you want people to say about you? How would they describe you? What would they say you did during your time on earth? Did you make a difference in any one's life? Were you focused on making an impact? Did you do all the things you said you would do? Did you live a full life? Did you have a vision before you? Did you fully enjoy the value of each day?

Or did you live a life of regret, visionless, going through the motions without much thought about your purpose? Did you waste days watching television, gossiping, scrolling through social media for countless hours, pushing the snooze button, and letting opportunities pass you by?

Twenty years after that life-changing moment in high school, I returned to that assignment as I sat at my keyboard and began writing my new, revised obituary. I sat in my guest bedroom in 2006 with nothing but a laptop and a head full of questions, ideas, thoughts, and dreams. I wrote my full name at the top with my birthdate underneath (but no "expiration date" attached...I'm not prophesying anything!). I began writing exactly how I want to be remembered as a person, a wife, a mother, a daughter, a friend, a leader, and a world changer.

I wrote big, audacious, crazy, out-of-the-realm-of-possibility paragraphs that immediately brought up questions like, "How in the world...?" and "Who do you think you are?" But I didn't let that stop me from dreaming. I let my imagination soar and my aspirations exceed what I was currently capable of doing.

Something remarkable happened. It caused a flame in me to ignite and come alive like no other exercise I had ever done before. It was a completely different mental challenge than writing down my goals for the year of paying off debts and losing five pounds. When you imagine coming to the end of your life and your closest family and friends are describing how you lived it, you'll want them saying more than, "She finally paid off that student loan!" No, this exercise will awaken dreams in you that you never thought possible.

What you're doing is defining success for *you*. As creepy as it sounds, you're writing what you want printed in black and white on the back pages of your local (or global) newspaper for all the world to read. Why not write something that inspires others to get up off the couch, make a difference with their lives, and truly live their definition of success.

It's Your Turn

Now, it's your turn. Write the obituary you want to have written about you. Use the same journal you're using during your prayer and meditation time. You don't have to write this all in one sitting. You probably won't. Take your time with this. It may take days or weeks of thinking and rewriting, scribbling or deleting. Think as big as you can. Dream as far as you can. Imagine as broad as possible. You are setting the course for your destiny with every word.

With extreme humility and enormous gratitude, I can honestly say that nearly everything I wrote in my far-fetched obituary in the year 2006 is nearly all achieved. Don't worry. That doesn't mean that my time is up. It simply means that I've revised my eulogy, added paragraphs to my life, and stretched myself even further to live out everything Jesus died to give me. And He wants that for you, too.

Earl Nightingale famously said, "First, we have to define success and here is the best definition I've ever been able to find: 'Success is the progressive realization of a worthy ideal.' A success is the school teacher who is teaching because that's what he or she wants to do. A success is the entrepreneur who starts his own company because that was his dream—that's what he wanted to do. A success is the salesperson who wants to become the best salesperson in his or her company and sets forth on the pursuit of that goal. A success is anyone who is realizing a worthy predetermined ideal, because that's what he or she decided to do…deliberately."[121]

You get the chance today, right now, to deliberately decide your own definition of success, and then hold yourself accountable for living it. In essence, go write your dream obituary...and then live it.

2. Define an unsuccessful life for you.

As equally important for fueling your motivation, you need to paint a vivid picture of life with no improvement beyond today. As discouraging as it sounds, this exercise can be quite motivating.

I will never forget in 2009 when I was contemplating my future and nearly allowing fear to stop me dead in my tracks.

I had gotten comfortable as the CEO for my father's ministry for the past six years. I loved what I was doing serving him in ministry. What once stretched me beyond my capacity had become a position I eventually held with more ease. I thoroughly enjoyed working behind the scenes, meeting with my teams, brainstorming, ghostwriting, and sitting behind my beautiful black desk in Crowley, Texas. But I knew God was calling me to minister and to reach more people than my co-workers at staff meetings within the four walls of our headquarters. I had been ministering a bit, but I had reached a crossroads in my life where it was either go halfway or go all-in.

God doesn't let us get too comfortable for too long. He's constantly stretching us to new heights. But comfort and convenience run the lives of unsuccessful people. The thought of stepping out of my comfort zone to minister on stage, to write books, and to be in the public eye in a greater degree was frightening. I felt a tug inside that I needed to launch my ministry on a wider scale, but the thought of hiring my own staff, paying salaries, buying equipment, leasing offices, not to mention opening myself up to more criticism, more opinions, and more exposure was paralyzing me with fear.

There was a struggle between what I thought I should do versus what I wanted to do. I liked being comfortable. I liked my nest, so-to-speak, at my dad's ministry where I had grown into a leader. I felt blessed getting to serve my dad. What was wrong with staying cozy there? On the other hand, what if I missed out on what God had called me to do because I was too afraid to step out?

Finally, to end the battle in my mind, I decided to paint a vivid picture of my life 10 years into the future if I didn't change a thing. I have to be honest with you, this exercise in my imagination was just as eye-opening and life-altering as writing my dream obituary. I added up my age 10 years into the future, my wedding anniversary, my daughter's age, as well as my years of employment with my father's organization.

On that same laptop, in the same guest bedroom where I wrote my obituary a few years earlier, I drew the opposite scenario of my life as if nothing changed from 2009 to the year 2019. I typed it in high-definition, leaving nothing out so I couldn't second guess myself any longer. I went through my routine from the moment I woke up (in the same bedroom), went to the same gym, drove the same roads, sat at the same desk, ate at the same restaurant, worked with some of the same people, and lived the exact same life.

I imagined my daughter coming to visit me (she would be out of school by then) and meeting me for lunch at my same lunchroom. I described how I felt as we caught up on each other's lives; however, I didn't have much to tell her because nothing had changed. When I imagined her hugging me goodbye, I went back up to my office, and I was embarrassed, ashamed, and felt like I had let her down because I didn't live my dreams as I always encouraged her to do. Again, it wasn't that my life was so bad, it was about knowing God was calling me to do more, but I disobeyed.

I imagined running into my former co-workers from 2009, and I was disappointed in myself. I remember typing out how I didn't want to see them because I knew that I had let them down. They knew I had potential to do more, but I had chosen comfort over my calling.

I'll spare you all the laborious thoughts that raced through my mind as I painted this picture. By the end of it, I will never forget writing these words: "Rodney and I are comfortable. We live in a nice house. I earn a good salary. We go on a Hawaiian vacation every summer. But how many scrapbooks can I make of Rodney and Terri on the beach? I'm comfortable, but I'm miserable. I know God had more for my life, but I was too scared. I'm disappointed in myself. I'm full of regret."

198

As I typed the words flowing out of me without much forethought, my eyes were wide open to the harsh reality that I had to shake off the complacency, face my fears, and step boldly out of my comfort zone into my destiny!

That picture of an unsuccessful life fueled me to never let that be the eulogy spoken of me at my funeral. I challenge you to invest the time it takes to sit quietly with yourself and paint a vivid, play-by-play description of your day-to-day life 10 years from right now if you don't adapt these daily successful habits.

What does your life look like as you add another decade assuming you choose to stop and settle where you are today? Are you satisfied? Are you comfortable? Are you disappointed in yourself? Do you feel that you had greater potential than what you tapped? Are you embarrassed to run into your former co-workers seeing how they moved on and went for their dreams but you're still in the same spot a decade later? What do you talk about at dinner 10 years from now? What do your children say you're doing with your life? Do they brag on you as their inspiration and their role model?

The good news is, it's not 10 years from now. It's only today, and you get to choose how you want to be remembered and how you want to live the next decade of your life.

3. Know your why.

The reasons why you want to achieve something are extremely motivating in keeping you disciplined. But they can't just be superficial reasons; they need to be deep and profound as we saw when you take the time to write your dream obituary.

As much as I love vision boards and showing you how to live your dreams, I don't simply believe that a successful life is solely about reaching all your goals and checking them off. If that were the case, then why would comedic actor Robin Williams hang himself in a mansion in

Beverly Hills surrounded by goals achieved, awards earned, and money in the bank? As heartbreaking as it was to hear that news and as much as I loved watching him excel in his craft, he lacked something in his life to bring him true joy and fulfillment.

A Clipboard and Keys

On July 9, 2003, I found my why. When people ask me how I stay motivated or if I ever get tired of my routine year after year, I always respond with my story of a clipboard and keys.

It was 5:30 in the morning that hot, July day in Texas, and I was out walking in my neighborhood. I was still filled with anxiety and guilt from my past, and battling my worth and value to even have a dream in my heart. As I made my routine lap around the cul-de-sac, I prayed quietly under my breath asking God once again to forgive me for my awful sins. But this time, something happened. In a vision, I saw myself standing at the foot of the cross, and I looked up and saw the feet of Jesus. Blood was dripping from His feet and landing on the top of my head. Inside, I clearly heard the Lord speak these words to me, "I'm washing the memories away," as His blood covered my head.

Next, the blood of Jesus flowed down to my heart, and I heard Him whisper, "I am the Healer of the brokenhearted." His crimson blood poured all the way down to the bottom of my feet, and the Lord said, "The residue of sin is gone from you."

The next thing I saw was a big arm reach down from Heaven and hand me a clipboard. With it, I heard these words, "This is an assignment on your life." Then, the other arm reached down and handed me keys and explained, "And here are the keys to the Kingdom of Heaven to help you fulfill your assignment."

What exactly did that life-altering vision mean and how could something so bizarre and imaginary fuel my motivation for decades? Well, for one, God was vividly showing me proof that the blood of

Jesus washes our sins away. He was offering me supernatural amnesia of my past! He showed me that He can heal every broken place in our lives and that we don't have to be reminded of our past ever again.

The clipboard was a clear picture proving that you and I have an assignment by God, a future, a calling, a purpose for being born. The keys to walking out that purpose are clearly written in God's Word, and I've been sharing them with you throughout this book and in each message I teach.

Since that pivotal moment that summer morning, I found a Bible verse that illustrates what I saw and provides my why for staying focused. John 17:4 says, "I glorified You on earth by completing down to the last detail what you assigned me to do" (MSG). That is the verse I am driven to accomplish. I see every person being given a clipboard from Heaven with your name written across the top, and there is an assignment God is going to hold you accountable for fulfilling during your time on earth.

In the words of John Bevere, I am "driven by eternity." My ultimate goal in life is to stand before God and say, "I did exactly what You assigned me to do down to the last detail." My mission in life is to go all over the world teaching the keys to fulfilling the life assignment on your clipboard so you can stand before God and hear Him say, "Well done, good and faithful servant."

Let this drive you to get up each morning and practice your disciplines and habits because it's leading you closer and closer to the overall assignment God has for your life...and He's going to hold you accountable for fulfilling it. Let this verse speak to you personally: "Perhaps this is the moment for which you have been created" (Esther 4:14).

3 Commands for You Today

I love the story in the Bible of the guy laying by the pool of Bethesda.

Apparently, the sick and disabled people would lay by this pool waiting for an angel to stir the water and the first to enter would be healed. John 5 records when Jesus noticed this one invalid laying by the pool and realized that he had been in that same position for 38 years. He asked the poor man, "Are you sure you want to get well?"

Think about this. Why would Jesus ask an obviously handicapped man if he wanted to get well? Of course, this man wants to be healthy and whole, living a normal life. Why would Jesus need to ask such an obvious question? Well, the reason he asked is because *nothing had changed in 38 years*! Allow your mind to process the numbers. Nearly four decades of idleness...just waiting.

When Joyce Meyer teaches from this passage, she makes me laugh with her version of the invalid man's whiny, self-pitying response, "Yes, but while I am waiting (for someone to come and get me), someone else always gets in front of me." In her sarcastic humor, she says, "In 38 years, I could at least wiggle myself over to the pool and fall in!"

My question for you (and I had to answer this myself) is this: *Are you sure* you want what you say you want? Are you sure you want to be debt free? Are you sure you want to lose that weight? Are you sure you want that job or promotion? Are you sure you want to start a business or have your own ministry? Are you sure you want to open a dance studio, daycare center, orphanage, or catering business? Why? Because nothing has changed in 5 years, 10 years, 17 years, or even 38 years.

What was Jesus' response to this sick man who had been waiting to be healed for so long? You might imagine that He said something along the lines of, "Oh bless your heart. You have been through so much. Let me help you up and get you the proper care you need."

No, in his heart of compassion, Jesus gave the man three commands:
1. Get up.
2. Pick up your bed.
3. Walk.

In comparison, what could Jesus be saying to *you* today?

Get up! Pick up your guitar and play!
Get up! Pick up your resume and get that dream job!
Get up! Pick up your passport and go on the mission field!
Get up! Pick up your courage and open your business!
Get up! Pick up your bottom and go to the gym!
Get up! Pick up your license and sell homes!
Get up! Pick up your manuscript and write that bestselling book!

In other words, nobody else can do this for you. You have to pick yourself up! You have to make the decision to not wallow around another year, complaining about the conditions, waiting for somebody to help you. You have to decide not to come to the end of your life with regret. Les Brown says, "If you fall down, try to land on your back. As long as you can look up—you can get up!"

4. Desire success more than any competing desire.

> **"Desire: the starting point of**
> **ALL achievement."**
> **- Napoleon Hill**

Have you ever played that old machine at a carnival or an arcade room where it measures your passion? You squeeze the handle, and the red light goes up and down rotating between: uncontrollable, hot stuff, passionate, burning, sexy, wild, mild, harmless, or clammy. You hope it lands on something "steamy" in front of your friends! That game (as silly as it is) is designed to rate your passion. Wouldn't it be great if we could measure the passion level for our dreams as easily? Drop a quarter in the machine, squeeze the handle and see what your odds for success are. Honestly, I believe we can measure our passion that easily. "How?" You ask. By the results in our lives.

The number one motivating factor behind the achievement of your dreams is desire. In other words, how badly do you want what you say you want? Because your results prove it. How badly you desire a thing dictates *your behavior* and reflects the *level of effort* you are willing to put forth.

The bottom line is: if you desire something badly enough, you will get it! If you really want to lose weight, you will. If you really want to get out of debt, you will. If you really want to start a business, you will. If you really want to go on a European cruise, you will. If you really want to write a book, you will. If you really want to save $10,000, you will. If you really want to draw closer to God, you will. It's simple. We do what we truly desire to do.

If a guy really wants to go out with a girl, he will call. He will text. He will show up. He will do these things because he desires her. If he doesn't desire her badly enough, he won't call, he won't text, he won't show up. In other words, move on. People do what they truly desire to do. It may sound harsh, but it's the truth.

That's why you see a woman who's been married for 10 years, battling with her weight for the past seven. Then suddenly, she goes through a painful divorce and within months, she's lost 25 pounds! What happened? Her attention shifted. Her motivations changed. How did she finally get victory over her body? Desire! She strongly desired to remarry, or to make her ex jealous, or realized how valuable she was. Whatever the reason, desire is the number one motivating factor behind change. Weak desires bring weak results. Strong desires bring strong results.

We've discovered throughout this book that you are where you are right this minute because of you, your choices, your desires, and your level of commitment. Because of your level of desire, you have what you have at this moment in your life. That could mean a fit body, a healthy savings account, a successful career, a strong family, and an intimate relationship with God...or not.

I know a 15-year-old girl who had a strong desire to go on a costly mission trip to Europe. She was so inspired by the vision of this outreach that she set a goal to raise the $7,000 required, somehow-someway. She made a vision board with photos of all the European countries she would be touring (Italy, France, England, and Germany). Then, she wrote the seemingly impossible amount of $7,000 to raise in one year's time, but she had the faith to believe and a strong, compelling desire to achieve it. She began looking for every opportunity she could find to raise money. She had a garage sale, cleaned houses, taught dance lessons, babysat kids, made clothing and sold it, asked for money, and other various jobs. This teenage girl with no full-time job raised $7,000 in 11 months! How? Desire!

Now, think about a credit card or student loan you may be carrying for three years paying the minimum amount of $25.00 on a $5,000 balance that looks impossible to pay off. Why is it taking so long? Weak desires bring weak results. When you get determined to pay off your debts and start building your financial savings account, you will surprise yourself by the creative ideas you'll find to get debt-free! Strong desires bring strong results.

How do you elevate your desires to truly go after your dreams? You change your desires by changing what you give attention to. Stop looking at what you're giving up and focus on where you're going. For example, if you have a desire to start saving money, but you also have a competing desire to go shopping, then you must give more attention to your goal of financial security than you do going to the mall or browsing your favorite shops online. In other words, give attention to reading books about financial freedom, listen to podcasts, play audiobooks, look at your savings goal on your vision board, remind yourself of people you know who were left with nothing, widows or widowers who died and left their spouses with all the bills and no savings account or life insurance. When you give your financial goal massive amounts of attention, your desire to achieve it will be unquenchable.

Get this phrase ingrained in your mind: You change your desires by changing what you give attention to. Desire is the motivating factor behind change. Do what you need to do to elevate your desire. Put your goals on the screen saver of your phone, the dash of your car, the screen on your computer. Surround yourself with new desires. When you desire something with great intensity, you will get it!

5. Don't compare your ambition with anyone else.

It is *vitally* important on the road to your dreams that you do not compare your new success habits with anyone else. You will, most likely, look around at the people closest to you and observe them sleeping in until 9 a.m. while you force yourself up before the sun. You'll witness them binge watching the latest show on Netflix while you're watching a Ted Talk. While they're dancing around in the morning, jamming out to *your* favorite beats, you're listening to another motivational podcast. While they're posting on Facebook, you're finishing off another book. While they're going to the mall, you're going to the gym. It's not fair, is it? Or is it?

I love Joyce Meyer's powerful reminder from a time in her life when she questioned why she was required to work so hard when others around here weren't. The Lord reminded her of her audacious dreams with this question, "Joyce, you've asked Me for a lot. Do you want it or not?"

I have held onto those words every time self-pity tries to consume my thought life. When I start to feel sorry for myself for all the hours I invest in my daily five while others are napping, swimming, shopping, and surfing the web, that's when I am reminded of my *clipboard and keys* (aka my assignment).

Whatever God has called you to do, it's going to require a lot out of you. I would imagine, since you're reading a book like this, you've asked the Lord for some pretty big dreams, and it's going to require a pretty big commitment. Do you want it or not?

When you are tempted to compare your life to theirs (whoever they are), your habits to theirs, your dreams to theirs, you have to remember, God hasn't told them what He's told you. They may not share the same drive, aspiration, or self-motivation as you, so don't expect it. In fact, let it encourage you that you're not like the average person. You're no longer mediocre, second-rate, average, or ordinary. You're exceptional, phenomenal, tremendous, and extraordinary.

You're on the path to success and gearing up for greatness. God is preparing you privately so He can use you publicly.

We are reminded in Galatians 6:9, "Let us not be weary in well doing: for in due season we will reap if we faint not." All your hard work, early hours, commitment, and self-motivation will pay off. If you truly want to live the life of your dreams, it will always require four little words from you: *a little bit more*! Successful people do what's expected of them—plus a little bit more!

Charles Kendall Adams said, "No student ever attains very eminent success by simply doing what is required of him; it is the amount of excellence of what is over and above the required that determines greatness."[122]

The difference between ordinary and extraordinary is that little word: extra! William Arthur Ward's poem, "While Others Are", nails the description of the road to success:

Believe while others are doubting
Plan while others are playing
Study while others are sleeping

Decide while others are delaying
Prepare while others are daydreaming
Begin while others are procrastinating
Work while others are wishing
Save while others are wasting
Listen while others are talking
Smile while others are frowning
Commend while others are criticizing
Persist while others are quitting

6. Declare a fast.

If you've battled for years with a lack of self-discipline, then I highly recommend that you take this issue to the Lord in prayer and declare a fast. There is something powerful that happens when we call on Heaven and make a commitment to fast before the Lord.

Especially when you've battled destructive habits (overeating, gossiping, overspending, laziness, gambling, eating too much sugar, etc.) and you want to break the habit at once, you need to consider going on a fast. Ask the Holy Spirit for guidance. Pray daily and call on Heaven to give you the supernatural strength to break the power of any addiction in Jesus' Name.

Be clear on why you're fasting. In this case, it's to develop a lifestyle of discipline and good habits in your life. The type of fast you choose is completely up to you. You could go on a full fast in which you only drink liquids, or you may choose to do the "Daniel fast," based on Daniel who abstained from sweets, meats, and any drink but water. Many times, I design my own fast which involves refraining from specific foods that I crave. Jentzen Franklin says, "If it means something to you, it means something to God."

Choose a starting date on the calendar and decide exactly how long you want to fast. You can fast as long as you like. Some people fast 1–3 days, 21 days, or a full 40 days. Keep your commitment to the Lord and to yourself. When you do, you are no longer trying to be disciplined in your own strength; you now have Almighty God giving you supernatural strength.

I highly recommend reading Jentzen Franklin's book, *Fasting*, to gain a true understanding of the reasons and benefits of going on a fast. Fasting is truly a prerequisite to experiencing major breakthroughs in your life. It is not recommended to do strenuous exercises when you're fasting all foods. So, be wise. Educate yourself in fasting, and be aware of how much physical activity you can afford to do.

Pray as often as you can throughout the day. Get away from the normal distractions as much as possible. Keep your heart and mind set on seeking God's face. Let me give you this little piece of advice: Never again say that you are undisciplined! Think of that statement like cursing because it is cursing your own future. Start declaring, "I am disciplined in my spirit, soul, and body."

Being self-motivated is one of the most essential traits to living your dreams. Though most people acknowledge its importance, few maintain it. The fact that you are inspired to be more disciplined, to improve your routine, and to keep yourself motivated is a sign of inner strength and desire. As your discipline grows, so will your confidence and self-esteem. The most successful people in the world are self-motivated and have self-discipline.

Don't strive for perfection; strive to complete your assignment...down to the last detail.

MY DAILY ROUTINE

Kelli Finglass
Director of the Dallas Cowboys Cheerleaders
Daily 5:

1. Each evening: I layout my wardrobe, I pre-pack my work bag, my outfit, charge my phone, and load my car.

2. By eliminating any morning time wasters the evening before, I cherish my quiet time in the morning.

3. I listen to a podcast.

4. I read a devotional. I MUST consume something positive, energizing, or refreshing before I look at email or start social media.

5. To stay focused on my priorities and professional goals, I have categorized my days into 7 to-do lists. Anything that needs to get done hits one of these lists. I just assign it to a specific day in my reminders app in my phone.

10

DON'T BREAK
THE CHAIN!

There's a story about a tribe of Aborigines in Australia who perform a special rain dance. This tribe, however, has something that sets them apart from other tribes. It *always* rains when this group performs. Well, you can't argue with results. Because of their phenomenal track record, they're able to charge the most money for their services.

One season in particular when farmers were experiencing a tremendous drought, one of them suggested each farmer put their money together and hire these extraordinary rain dancers. The farmers were desperate for rainfall. So, they agreed.

Sure enough, the tribe danced and suddenly, the drought came to an end, the clouds darkened, and the downpour came. Inquisitive, one of the farmers asked, "What is it about your tribe that makes it rain every time? What are you doing differently than the other tribes?"

The rain dancer simply said, "We just dance *until* it rains."

And there you have it. They dance until it rains. The others quit before the rainfall! They could have gotten the same results, had the same reputation, and demanded the same high fees, but they quit before they saw success.

How long do you persist toward your dreams? Until it happens. How long do you push yourself to get up each morning and commit to your routine? Until it becomes a habit.

> **"So let's not get tired of doing what is good. At just the right time we will reap a harvest of blessing if we do not give up." - Galatians 6:9, NLT**

Anyone who has achieved great success has learned to have stickability. In other words, they stick with things when they don't see progress just as much as they stick with things when they exceed their expectations. You could say that they're *glued* to their goals. It means if they have a goal, a dream, a vision, then they stick to it *until* it happens! I believe a great deal of our success is our ability to stay consistent and committed until we see success.

For example, in 2008, I started a little eight-minute podcast on YouTube. We received a total of 8,000 views the entire first year! To put that in perspective, that's about 22 people watching per day. Less than two dozen people were interested in what I had to say. But I kept preparing messages week after week, recording them, and uploading them online all year long.

I continued the process in 2009. That's 104 weekly podcasts, around 832 minutes, or 14 hours of content over the course of two years. By then, the amount of views I had in two years was less than the size of a crowd Justin Bieber sings to in *one single night*!

In 2010, I continued. We gained a few more views. We kept going week after week, year after year in 2011, 2012, 2013 and beyond. Nearly 50 hours of content was developed and uploaded and finally, it started to really take off!

It took us six years to gain one million views. Now, there are times we see one million views every six weeks. Our views can be as much as 35,000 per day. As I mentioned, the entire first year, we had 8,000 views total. Now, we have 8,000 views before lunch each day!

"How?" You might ask. "What did you do differently to see such growth?" We stuck with it. We were glued to its success. We continued until we saw progress. Today, everywhere I travel to speak in conferences—Holland, Germany, France, Switzerland, and across the USA—people tell me, "I found you on YouTube." Last year alone, our organization shipped resources (books, audios, and kits) to 83 countries. How in the world does anyone in Djibouti know who I am? YouTube. That little eight-minute podcast that we stayed glued to *until* it succeeded has made its way to Djibouti!

What if I had given up in 2011 because I had not seen the response I dreamed of after three years? I am convinced our organization wouldn't be growing at the rate it is. I'm also convinced I wouldn't be given the extraordinary opportunities I've been given because of the notoriety the not-so-little-anymore podcast has afforded me.

Consistency is the key to success. What do you need to be glued to *until* it succeeds? I've had many people tell me through the years, "I'm gonna start a podcast." Then, they record three every other month and then stop for seven months, pick it back up again, and then complain that it's not growing. That's not glued. That's just a sticky mess. It's haphazard. It's unpredictable. It's a set up for failure.

People love predictability. They trust you when they can count on you. Consistency establishes your reputation. Business growth requires a track record of success. You can't establish a track record if you are constantly shifting gears or trying new tactics.

Every area of my life and my ministry that's succeeded has done so because I've stuck with things. Our Icing Women's Conference is another example. It launched in 2010 in Crowley, Texas with 325 women. I committed to hosting this event quarterly in the beginning to build momentum. I wanted people to get to know me, trust me, get used to my style and my messages, and feel comfortable inviting their friends to experience this event. I wanted to build a reputation and a relationship with our attendees. It was a lot of work for my team and for me to host this conference every three months, but we committed to it for several years. Then, I felt it was time to reduce it to twice a year. And now, it's an annual event in Fort Worth, Texas each fall that has grown to thousands of women coming from all over the world.

At times, it would have been more convenient to skip a year. It could have been tempting to stop altogether when 250 *fewer* people showed up one year than the year before. That's a significant drop in attendance when you're at that level. It would have been tempting to say, "I don't want to put myself through this responsibility. Let's take a break."

But consistency builds momentum in every area of life. Because we stuck with it, people across the globe have heard of Icing and tell me it's on their vision board to attend one day. They trust that it will be happening each year.

What have you started, then stopped, then started again, and stopped?

- Is it writing a blog?
- Practicing a language?
- Submitting articles to a magazine?
- Hosting live webinars?
- Hosting a conference?
- Making sales calls?
- Writing your manuscript?
- Weight loss program?
- Network marketing business?

Whatever it is, if you want to see success, stick with it *until* it succeeds.

I admit, it's easier to wish for the microwave-fast results, but the truth is, we have to use the crockpot approach when it comes to achieving our dreams and developing good habits. Like the famous tortoise and hare competition, slow and steady wins the race. You must stay dedicated for an *extended* period of time to gain momentum. There's no shortcut to excellence. Typically, if we don't see success instantly, we want to give up! How many creations in our lives would we not have today if the inventors had let time, setbacks, delays, and frustrations stop them?

Famous for Persistence

Take Macy's Department Store for example. Rowland H. Macy opened seven stores over a short period of time, and *all of them* were unsuccessful. In 1858, he opened his store in New York City and his first day of sales were $11.06. But he didn't let that convince him that it was time to throw in the towel. He continued. Today, Macy's Department Stores are located in 45 states across America. Let the iconic red star be a symbol of persistence and never giving up.

The first few Macy's parades were complete flops as well. The first parade was in Haverhill, Massachusetts on July 4, 1854, where his store was located at the time. His idea was to have a parade, and after the procession everyone would go into his store to shop. It sounded like a guarantee for success. Well, plans didn't unfold as he intended. The temperatures were boiling hot that day with only 100 spectators even attending the festivities, and then, they all wanted out of the squelching sun and proceeded home. Macy could have assumed the whole parade idea was a complete dud, but he continued. Even with its initial failure, he didn't let that deter his idea.[123]

Today, the Macy's Thanksgiving Day Parade is watched by about three and half million spectators standing along the streets of New York City plus approximately 50 million viewers watching it from their television sets across the country. I don't know about you, but I have benefited by R. H. Macy's stickability. Who will benefit because of your persistence in not giving up on your habits and your dreams?

Another famous example of persistence is Akio Morita. He thought he had a great idea to invent a rice cooker that, unfortunately, didn't cook the rice. It simply burned it. He sold less than 100 units of his great invention. This first setback didn't stop him as he pushed forward and created a little company called Sony. Morita and his team introduced the world to the tape recorder, the Walkman, the VCR, the PlayStation, and the list goes on. The first year they profited $300. Today, Sony's annual revenue is over $70 billion.[124] Have you ever enjoyed the fruit of Akio Morita's stickability? I think we all have.

On the Other Side

There's a statement that really shook me up after I began my five daily habits. I was driving to my office one typical day, incorporating the routine of listening to faith-building messages during my commute, and at the end of one of the messages, I heard this phrase: "Somebody in need is waiting on the other side of your obedience." The speaker repeated the phrase one more time: "Somebody in need is waiting on the other side of your obedience." And the message was over.

That sentence playing in my head over and over. I sat behind the wheel thinking, "Could anybody be waiting on me to get my act together, to get out of this funk, and get serious about my assignment and my dreams?" There were times I would convince myself, "Nah… nobody is waiting on me." But that statement never left me.

Today, when I receive testimonies from young women who have stopped cutting themselves because they found me on YouTube and my message resonated with them that God has a plan for their lives, or a young entrepreneur starts a business because they were inspired by my book to live their dreams, or an elderly man who saw me on TV one night realized that as long as he's alive God still has something for him to accomplish and contribute…. I can't help but think, "Somebody in need was waiting on the other side of my obedience."

Achieving your dreams isn't all about you. God needs you. People need you. Somebody is waiting on you. God is counting on you to stick with it!

The Seinfeld Strategy

I heard the funniest thing about late night infomercials. One of the major selling points for all infomercial products is how easily the item will fold up and slide under your bed or away in the closet. Why? Because that is exactly where it's headed. Everyone gets fired up watching someone else's success and the testimonials on the infomercial. But when we get our hands on it, we lose our commitment, so under the bed it goes.

To have the stickability we have talked about, you must have a plan for commitment. You have to develop a lifestyle of discipline. The Seinfeld Strategy is the perfect picture of a commitment to habits.

Jerry Seinfeld is one of the most successful comedians of all-time. He was the co-creator and co-writer of *Seinfeld*, the long-running sitcom which received numerous awards. However, what is extremely impressive about Seinfeld's career isn't just the awards, the earnings, or notoriety he achieved, it's his routine. His habits and his self-discipline are remarkable.

When a young comedian, Brad Isaac was starting out on the comedy circuit, he met Jerry Seinfeld backstage at a show. Isaac took the opportunity to ask Seinfeld if he had "any tips for a young comic."

Seinfeld graciously answered with advice that changed Brad Isaac's life and I believe will change yours if you let it. He said the way to be a better comic was to create better jokes, and the way to create better jokes was to *write jokes every single day* without fail. But his advice didn't stop there. He told Isaac to purchase a big wall calendar and display it where he'd see it every day. Plus a big, red marker. Then each day that Isaac wrote his jokes, he would get to draw a big red X over that day on the calendar.

"After a few days, you'll have a chain," said Seinfeld. "Just keep at it and the chain will grow longer every day. You'll like seeing that chain, especially when you get a few weeks under your belt. Your only job is to not break the chain."[125]

It didn't matter if he was motivated or not. It didn't matter if he was writing great jokes or not. It didn't matter if what he was working on would ever make it into one of his shows.

"Don't break the chain." Seinfeld said—I imagine him emphasizing each word and holding out the last syllable, the way he delivers his punchlines, but that's just me.

This approach has clearly worked for Jerry Seinfeld. According to *Forbes* magazine, he made $267 million dollars in 1998. Ten years later, even after the sitcom was over, Seinfeld was still bank rolling a reported $85 million per year. One simple but profound secret behind Seinfeld's notable success is consistency.

But it's not only for Jerry Seinfeld. It can be for you too, if you don't break the chain.

I came across a drummer who grew his YouTube channel to 500,000 subscribers. He said he started to see real growth when he decided to commit to posting a new video every Tuesday and every Thursday and then vowed to keep his schedule on the calendar! He promised himself without fail that he would not miss an upload. And today, he's enjoying the success of his consistency.

I want to share a few tips to help you "not break the chain" of your new routine.

MY DAILY ROUTINE

Nicole C. Mullen

Dove award-winning, Grammy-nominated singer/ songwriter

Daily 5:

1. Make my bed.

2. Read the Bible.

3. Pray.

4. Drink lots of water.

5. Walk and run for an hour.

1. Stick to your decisions—not your emotions.

> **"Commitment is doing the thing you said you'd do long after the mood you said it in has left you."**

If you said you're going to do it, do it. Joyce Meyer says, "If you live by your feelings, you'll live a life of devastation and misery. Don't let your feelings vote."

I read a conversation between a blogger and a successful author named Todd Henry. The blogger had come to terms with the fact that his writing was inconsistent and of questionable quality in contrast to Henry's valuable, consistent content. Trying to explain himself, the blogger asked the author, "Todd, what do you think about writing only when you feel motivated? I feel like I always do my best work when I get a spark of creativity or inspiration, but that only happens every now and then. I'm pretty much only writing when I feel like it, which means I'm inconsistent. But if I write all the time, then I'm not creating my best work."

"That's cool," Todd Henry replied. "I only write when I'm motivated too. I just happen to be motivated every day at 8 a.m."[126]

It's a given: You will have days when you don't *feel* like sticking with your routine. You must override those feelings with the firm decision to get up and do it. Why do you think Nike coined the phrase "Just do it"? Because every one of us has days when we want to "just skip it."

My dad says to practice having integrity with yourself. That means if you said you would make 5 sales calls every day, do it. If you said you would study a foreign language twice a week for 20 minutes, do it. If you said you would enroll in real estate classes, do it. If you said you were launching an annual women's conference, then commit to do it. If you said to the world, "I'm going to be hosting a Facebook Live once a week," do it. Even if 3 people are watching, keep your commitment. It builds credibility. It develops confidence in you. If you said you would read a book a month, do it. If you said you would attend a monthly Bible study, do it.

New York Times bestselling author, Debbie Macomber, has published more than 100 books, many of which have become bestsellers and made-for-TV movies. She also has a routine that's led her to her dreams. Every day, she wakes up at 4:30 a.m., reads her Bible, and writes in her journal. By 6:00 a.m., she swims laps in her swimming pool. By 7:30 a.m,, she answers her mail in her office. Between 10:00 a.m.– 4:00 p.m., she writes, regardless of how she feels! The result? She produces an average of three new books a year, and her books have sold over 60 million copies.[127]

It doesn't matter what you are trying to become better at, if you only do the work when you feel motivated, then you'll never be consistent enough to become an expert, a professional, or a dream achiever. You have to stick to your decision—especially when you don't feel like it! Professionals stick to their schedule; amateurs stick to their moods.

Note: If you miss a day or a week, don't feel like you have to start from scratch. Just pick yourself up and do it again.

2. Stick to your vision.

Software engineer, Brian Acton, wanted to be on the cutting edge of technology. Although he had 12 years of experience at Yahoo!, his dream job was to work for either Facebook or Twitter, but neither would hire him. After Twitter rejected him, he tweeted, "Got denied by Twitter HQ. That's ok. Would have been a long commute."

After being rejected from Facebook, he responded with another optimistic response by posting, "Facebook turned me down. It was a great opportunity to connect with some fantastic people. Looking forward to life's next adventure."

Although he was rejected by his two dream companies, he stuck with his desire to be involved with the latest technology. He decided to team up with a former co-worker at Yahoo! and began creating his own app, later called WhatsApp. Five years later, he sold that app to Facebook (of all companies) for a reported $19 billion![128]

No matter how many setbacks you have, rejections you encounter, or disappointments you experience, you have to stick with it! The reason I am so adamant about your stickability is because your discipline drives you to your dreams. And your dreams are a big part of the overall assignment God has placed on your life.

Accountable for Your Assignment

A statement I heard minister John Bevere make startled me but also lit a fire under my feet to fulfill my assignment. He said that when Judgment Day comes and we stand before God to give an account for our lives, we will *not* be held accountable for what we did on earth. At first that confused me, but I continued to listen as Bevere said, "You will be held accountable for what you were *called* to do on earth." In other words, what you do and what you are *called* to do could be two totally different outcomes.

God asks for your obedience to the assignment He's placed on your life; but He doesn't force it on you. You can choose to follow your God-given dreams or you can choose an average life, with little to no discipline and therefore little to no influence. But He will hold you accountable for what He has asked you to do. I don't know about you, but that makes me get serious about my daily disciplines.

Lindsay Roberts, wife of evangelist Richard Roberts, told an eye-opening story of her early days co-hosting a daily television show with her husband. She was so stricken with insecurity and shyness that she would literally vomit during the commercial breaks. She even hid a little bucket near her chair. She said, "I just felt worthless and unnecessary."

Eventually, she'd endured enough misery and told her husband, "Richard, I quit." Thirty minutes later, she heard the Lord speak to her, "Get to the studio." The only thing that scared Lindsay more than facing the television studio was disobeying God; so she obeyed. During the show, she heard the Lord say, "Someone is about to commit suicide. Tell them to call for prayer." She repeated on air exactly what she heard in her spirit. Sixteen people on the verge of ending their lives called and gave their hearts to the Lord! If that wasn't impactful enough, as Lindsay drove home, the Lord said to her, "If you hadn't obeyed and chosen to live by how you feel, I would have held you accountable for those sixteen lives."

Do whatever God is telling you to do. What are you shying away from because it frightens you or pushes you out of your comfort zone? What habits do you need to drop and which ones do you need to stick with? God needs you to make an impact in others' lives.

Maybe you feel unqualified. Unworthy. Uneducated. We all do. I'm certainly not qualified to be doing what I'm doing. I'm shy. I have to overcome insecurities every time I get on camera or walk on stage. I have to give myself a pep talk every day to stay focused. God doesn't call the qualified; He qualifies the called!

It Takes Grit to Not Quit

When I think of the grit it takes to pursue your dreams against all odds, I can't help but think of a guy named Milton. Milton dropped out of school at an early age and later became an apprentice with a printing company. Shortly thereafter, he was fired. He took another apprenticeship as a candy-maker.

After studying the business for four years, Milton started his own candy company in Philadelphia; unfortunately, it failed miserably. He tried again in Chicago, and when that location flopped, he opened another in New York only to watch it fail as well.

So, Milton gave up on his dreams, and we will never know who he could have become.

No! He refused to give up and developed such extreme stickability that his name is synonymous with chocolate. Milton Hershey built Lancaster Caramel Company with such a unique caramel recipe that he was able to sell the company for $1 million in the year 1900 (the equivalent to nearly $25 million today) and started a chocolate company called the Hershey Company. Milton Hershey was glued to his vision. And we get to enjoy the sweetness of his persistence![129]

I read where 90% of all first-time businesses fail. Ninety percent of all 2nd time businesses succeed; however, 80% of all people never try a second time![130] They lack the stickability it takes to find success.

Note one more important fact about Milton Hershey. He used a great deal of his wealth to build houses, churches, and schools benefiting the lives of others. Once again, we see that sticking to your dreams isn't solely for you. God sees a bigger picture, and He wants to use your dreams in ways you could never come up with on your own.

Stick with it and watch what God will do.

3. Stick to your calendar.

**"Don't prioritize your schedule;
schedule your priorities."
- Stephen Covey**

Priorities never stay put. We must build them into our lives. The reason we get our weekly podcast recorded and uploaded each week is because we schedule it ahead of time over the entire year. Once dates are on our calendar, it's in writing, and it gets done. It's not up for debate. We will tape the podcast. We will upload it. We will stick with it.

We schedule our priorities. Our team meetings, our conferences, my writing time, etc. We block off time on the calendar or it won't get done.

The great motivator Zig Ziglar said when he was a salesman, he had never even been in the top 5,000 in his sales company. In order to change that, he made a commitment to himself to work on a regular schedule and to believe in himself.

"At exactly 9:00 every morning, without fail, rain or shine, cold or hot," said Ziglar, "I was knocking on somebody's door." His wife would ask him, "Where are you going?" And he would always answer, "I've got an appointment." He never told her his appointment was with himself to be knocking on doors. Once he got committed to his schedule, he finished second place out of 7,000 sales people.[131]

Successful people never go to bed without planning the day ahead. Nearly every self-help guru or success coach imaginable recommends this productive tool to increase your success. It's easy to get off track when you don't have a written plan. You wake up not knowing what you need to accomplish and wind up wasting hours with no focus.

John Maxwell says, "I plan my calendar 40 days at a time. When I get ready to approach a day, I have the whole thing laid out. Hour by hour. It's a rare day that I get up in the morning wondering what I will be doing that day—even when on vacation."[132]

The truth is what you do the day before matters just as much as what you do each morning. In fact, without a plan in place, you have no clarity about what you're trying to get done on any given day. No doubt you'll be busy, but probably not productive.

What gets planned, gets done. This is a total game changer in establishing your new habits. I am a strong advocate of not only planning your life dreams and goals, but planning how you'll spend the next hour. Even if that means taking a nap, plan it.

I never end a day without planning my next day. Having structure in your morning is essential to your success. Invest 10-15 minutes before you go to bed to establish the exact time you will wake up, how long you will read, what time you will work out, when you will spend time in prayer or journaling. If you commit to this plan, you will eliminate excuses, increase your productivity, and succeed on purpose.

Wake up with determination and go to sleep with satisfaction that you did what you set out to do. Spend a little time each evening giving yourself clear goals for the next day. Then, wake up and tackle the list.

Remember what gets scheduled, gets done.

4. Stick to your habits.

When people ask motivational speaker, Dan Lier, what the key to success is, he answers, "consistency." He says, "If it's not a habit or a hobby, it's not going to happen. The key is to make it a habit."[133]

I mentioned in Chapter 4 how I had to make reading a daily habit because it wasn't a hobby. The more I committed to this daily habit, the more I began to desire it. Now, I crave it. I want to be reading a good book. That's what I look forward to on vacations. Jack Canfield "read over 3,000 books by a *simple dose every day*."

We know now that successful people have successful habits. Habits are the foundation for a successful life. They compound over time, and one day, you realize you've drastically changed. But it all began with a simple change in your routine.

I heard someone say that one of the reasons it's so hard to stick to daily progress is because we get used to watching a movie that shows people meet, fall in love, get married, have kids, achieve success, all squished into two hours! Movies show us people who conquer the world, slay dragons, start businesses and defeat avatars in the same amount of time it takes you to do laundry! But in reality, it takes day-to-day consistency.

John Maxwell uses the illustration of swinging an ax to cut down a tree. Maxwell says, "Picture a tree in your backyard that needs to be cut down. If you grab an ax and take five good swings at the tree each day, eventually you will chop it down. It may take a month to fell a small tree, while a big tree may take years to topple over. The size of the tree isn't the issue; the real question is whether or not you diligently take five swings at it every day."[134]

Each day that you own your mornings and you commit to getting up and practicing your daily disciplines, you will see your limits fall, your challenges topple over, and your breakthrough emerge!

A Little Change Adds Up to Big Results

Early in our marriage, Rodney and I started saving our change. A little at a time, we would throw a few pennies, a nickel, a couple of quarters into a giant Coca-Cola bottle-shaped bank. Months went by, and it looked like we probably had about $7.00 saved. But we kept on and kept on and kept on. When I was expecting our baby girl, we were in desperate need of extra finances to pay the doctor and hospital bills.

We had no health insurance at the time and all extra funds were spent on my burrito fixes, Dairy Queen blizzards, and stretchy pants. In dire need of resources, we had a random thought when we glanced at our piggy bank in the corner, "Let's take the change up to the bank and see how much money we've saved."

Before we entered the bank, we played a guessing game. I said, "Oh, it's probably around $78." Rodney guessed higher, around $92 in coins. Boy, were we surprised when the bank teller poured our coin collection into the bin and we watched it spin around for several minutes then spit out a receipt of $372.00 in change! We were shocked to discover that our little habit of tossing coins into a coke bottle provided more than enough for our first doctor bill. What am I saying? Change adds up little by little to outstanding results.

It's the same in your life: Every bit of change you make adds up! Every morning that you stick to your habits and don't break the chain adds up!

Darren Hardy, author of *The Compound Effect*, asks, "Have you ever been bitten by an elephant? How about a mosquito? It's the little things that bite you."[135] Habits can seem like such a little thing, but added up on a daily basis, they can make or break your success.

Think about Elijah in the Bible when he went to Mount Carmel and prayed to God that the drought would end and that rain would come. While he was praying, he asked his servant to go look towards the sea for a rain cloud. The servant came back and said, "There is nothing in the sky, Elijah."

Elijah asked him to go check again. There was nothing. But Elijah wouldn't give up. "Check again," he commanded his servant. "Clear skies everywhere," the servant continued to report. Seven times Elijah repeated this scene, adamant that God would be faithful to his cry. On the seventh report, the servant came back and said, "There is a small cloud, the size of a man's hand."

That's all Elijah needed to hear. He told his servant, "Run to Ahab and tell him the downpour is coming!"[136] Meanwhile, the little cloud grew bigger and bigger, and the sky got darker and darker. The wind started to blow, and the showers began to fall. The drought was over. The breakthrough came because he refused to give up.

Every time you get up and go read, you're making progress. Every time you keep your commitments, you're making progress. Every time you tell your feelings to shut up, you're making progress.

Every time you're getting closer to your breakthrough.

Don't back down. Don't stop halfway. Don't allow a seeming lack of results to stop you from plugging away. It's compounding. It's getting you closer. Don't quit now!

5. Stick to it until...

**"Success is the sum of small efforts
repeated day in and day out."
- Robert Collier**

There are so many thoughts and studies on how long it takes to form a habit. I have shared repeatedly how I began my lifestyle of discipline by committing to practice my five habits for 21 days. This mindset was based on something I heard in college from a psychology professor who claimed it only takes three weeks to break an old habit and start a new one. In this book, I have challenged you with this same goal of going a solid 21 days (without exception) practicing your new habits. If you can only start with one habit, that's fine. Choose habit #1 (prayer/meditation) whether it's for 5 minutes or 20 minutes. Do it every day without skipping. Then for the next 21 days, don't stop the first habit but add habit #2 (read every day) and so on.

Let me explain that this goal is 21 days; however, the ultimate goal is forever. Start with the 21-day challenge of not breaking the chain then go for a full month and another month and so on.

Hint: The best way to start and maintain a new habit is to do it at the same time each day. That's why I practice all five of my habits in the morning, as do most successful people. They are pretty much at the exact same hour each day no matter where I'm traveling in the world. It becomes engrained in your subconscious mind over time until there's no need to even remind yourself. You automatically do it.

I recently read Strategist Marissa Bracke's "Three Day Rule of Effective Habits" where she said, "If you don't want it as a habit, don't do it for three days straight. And if you do want it as a habit, don't skip it for three days straight." Typically, we can adjust to skipping a day or two of a new habit (though I don't recommend it), but once we take three days off, it's no longer a break. We're starting a pattern. And once it's a pattern, we fall right back into a bad habit.

Here is Bracke's Three Day Rule:
- One day is a breather.
- Two days is a break.
- Three days is a new pattern.[137]

Think of how it feels after a typical two-day weekend versus an extended three-day holiday off of work. It's just one extra day, but for some reason, it takes a lot more effort to get back in your groove. "One or two days? No problem. Three days? Suddenly you're feeling a little rusty. So goes the power of the three-day rule." says Bracke.

Of course, there are exceptions, but don't push it. Yes, give yourself rest if you're ill. Take holidays with your family. We all face disruptions from time to time, but you can still own your mornings and practice some of the habits as much as possible.

Even if you break the "Three Day Rule," don't give up. Don't call it quits. Don't burn this book. You can still pick up right where you left off on your calendar and keep going. Don't ever give up.

To learn how long it takes for a new habit to be so ingrained that it's second nature for you, psychologist Phillippa Lally and her team surveyed 96 people over a 12-week period. Her participants chose their preferred new habit and reported each day how automatic the new behavior felt. At the end of the twelve weeks, Lally analyzed the results finding the average time it took to adapt a new habit was 66 days.[138]

Don't let these numbers or studies startle or discourage you. The number itself isn't what's important. In fact, I've since seen habits taking everywhere from 18 days to 254 days to establish!

Just start with day number one and reward yourself with a big "X" on the calendar. Get up and do it again and again and again. Set a goal to not break the chain.

> **"The secret to breaking any bad habit**
> **is to love something**
> **greater than the habit."**
> **- Bryant McGill**

MY DAILY ROUTINE

"Real Talk" Kim

Pastor, conference speaker, author

Daily 5:

1. I get up and have my coffee with God (no coffee and no talkie with God is bad for my family).

2. I take my herbs and much needed juice.

3. Work on writing my new book every morning. Allot at least an hour every day.

4. I always start my day with prioritizing my list and of to-do's and mark them off as I'm done. Most important things first, not the urgent things.

5. I then shower and get my mohawk as high as I can get it (the higher the hair the closer to heaven) add a fabulous outfit and combat boots and GO FOR THE GOLD!

CONCLUSION

3 SIGNS YOU WILL BE SUCCESSFUL ONE DAY

"No discipline seems pleasant at the time, but painful. Later on, however, it produces a harvest of righteousness and peace for those who have been trained by it."
- Hebrews 12:11, NIV

First, I want you to know that I think you're amazing. Clearly, you are not average. You are not ordinary. You are truly exceptional. How do I know this? Because you've done what most people never do, yes, read books, but more than that, finish a book! I applaud you for going the extra mile, choosing the "car keys" over the "popcorn" and establishing a mindset that will truly elevate your entire life. You are way beyond where I was in 2002. You're like those successful people I studied and quoted throughout this book. You've already proven that you have the right mindset for greatness. You are disciplined. You are persistent. And you stick with things. But let's not stop here.

When you finish these last few pages of this book, you could do one of two things. You could be completely overwhelmed, close the book, put it on your bookshelf (or in the trash), and vow to never set your alarm again (much less get up and tackle five new habits)! And the truth is, I totally understand. I did that for 11 years. But I was miserable.

Or you could take action. You could have a meeting with yourself and decide to just start. Start small, start where you are, and commit to doing the five habits for five minutes each day which adds up to over 12 hours of personal growth each month! Think about it, only five minutes a day will still put you on the road to success. That's less time than it takes to boil an egg, fill up your car with gas, or put on mascara (if you wear as much as me). Your future, your life, your assignment is worth five minutes.

But it's entirely up to you.

Here's how I know if you have what it takes to be a success:

1. You make a quality decision to take responsibility for your life.

Everything starts with a decision. We know that your life today is a series of decisions you've made up to now. If you want the future to be different, you'll need to make better decisions. It starts by taking responsibility for where you are right this minute in your life (your health, your finances, your relationships, your lifestyle, your mindset) but also take responsibility to improve it.

Here are a few testimonies of people I know who have chosen to take action and change their lives by following the steps I've given you in this book.

- Carol realized at 56 years old she had saved nothing. She decided to take responsibility for where she was spending her money and how she wanted to retire one day. She started reading books about financial health and listening to messages to retrain her mindset. By the time she was 62, she had saved over $100,000.

- Debbie, a pastor in Denver, Colorado, struggled with her weight since having babies (and her babies were now in

233

their twenties). She made a decision to take responsibility for her poor health and lack of energy. She began listening to motivational teaching while walking 20 minutes a day. She said, "Out of 24 hours in a day, I can find 20 minutes to do something for my physical health." She's lost 26 pounds and kept it off because she made it a habit.

- Janan came to a conference I was speaking at and handed me a piece of paper with a list of things she accomplished in a short 18 months. It included passing her nursing exam, getting a $5,000 bonus, buying her dream car (a Jeep Wrangler), and losing 75 pounds. I asked, "What happened?" She said, "I got tired of watching everybody else go after their dreams while I sat by full of excuses. I made a vision board, subscribed to your podcasts, read every book you've written, and started taking action."

President John F. Kennedy didn't know how America could land a man on the moon. When he asked Dr. Warner Van Braun what it would take to build a rocket, carry a man to the moon and bring him safely back, Dr. Van Braun replied, "The will to do it."[139]

I believe you have the will to succeed. Now, it's time to follow up your will with firm decisions. Jack Canfield said, "There's only one person responsible for the quality of your life and that person is you. Everything about you is a result of your doing or not doing. Your income. Your debt. Your relationships. Your health. Your fitness level. Your attitudes and behaviors. Everything. That person you see when you look in the mirror is the chief architect of your life."[140]

I love this story about a man sitting at the kitchen table reading the morning paper. He promised his little girl that he would spend the day playing with her. So, his daughter came running downstairs eager to go outside and play. The father said, "Sweetheart, I just need a few more minutes." The daughter was antsy, tugging on her daddy's arm. Finally, the dad ripped out a picture of the world from the paper and tore it into tiny pieces across the table. He said, "Put this puzzle of the world together, and when you finish, we'll go outside and play." The little girl finished in less than three minutes!

Astonished, the dad said, "How did you do this so fast?" The daughter replied, "I dropped a piece on the floor and when I went under the table to get it, I looked up at the glass and could see a picture of a woman on the back of all the pieces," she explained. "So I turned all the pieces over and put the photo of the woman together." She concluded, "Once I put the woman together, the world just fell into place!"

Your world will come together as you put yourself together...and that begins when you take responsibility for where you are and where you're headed.

2. You practice self-discipline behind the scenes.

"Whenever you see a successful person, you only see the public glories, never the private sacrifices to reach them."
- Vaibhav Shah

What you do behind the scenes has more significance than what you do before a crowd. It's all part of the preparation for where God wants to take you. God always prepares us privately before he can use us publicly.

John Maxwell was teaching the importance of personal growth at a seminar when he agreed to do a Q&A at the end. A young university graduate stood up and asked, "John, I love your leadership principles.

I just wish I had somebody to lead. Where should I start?" Maxwell responded, "Good question. Start with YOU." He told the young man, "Before you can lead anyone else, you must learn to lead yourself."[141] And that takes place behind the scenes day after day.

A good exercise is to imagine a teenager asking, "Can I shadow you for the next five days and watch your habits?" What would they see about your daily life (your routine, your rituals, your habits) that would motivate them to want to be more like you?

What if they witnessed you rising early, spending quality time alone and journaling your thoughts in prayer. Next, they see you pick up a personal growth book, read it, highlight it, make notes in the margins for 20 minutes, and then you move on to declaring your dreams and goals out loud as you view your vision board of aspirations. You finish off your morning by listening to a motivational teaching while you jog for 30 minutes around the neighborhood. By 8:00 a.m., you say, "Now, let's get to work." Do you think they would be impressed, inspired, surprised, motivated? Clearly, they would.

I never dreamed in 2002 when I started these five habits that they would not only get me out of a rut but into a routine that would change the course of my life. What you do privately is more important than what people see publicly.

There's a story about a lady at a market place that ran into the famous artist, Picasso, and she asked with excitement, "Picasso, can you draw me a portrait?"

He said, "Sure, I will." He reached for a pen and paper and within 30 seconds, he sketched a portrait of this lady! He handed it to the woman and said, "That will be $30,000."

"How can you charge me $30,000 when it only took you 30 seconds to do that?" She shouted.

To which Picasso replied, "Ma'am, it took me 30 years to be able to do that in 30 seconds!"

Every day that you invest in yourself, you're becoming more and more valuable to the marketplace and to those around you.

In the Bible, we see David kill a lion and a bear in private with nobody watching, but that prepared him to kill Goliath in public with everybody watching. What you do behind the scenes (your daily five) is all preparation for where God wants to take you. Preparation time is never wasted time.

"Success doesn't occur because of a one-time event," said Darren Hardy, "It's through a continuum of mundane, unsexy, unexciting, and sometimes difficult daily disciplines compounded over time." If you want to be successful, it demands an investment of your time…consistently."[142] Always remember, people are rewarded in public for what they practice in private.

> **"Do not despise the day of**
> **small beginnings."**
> **- Zechariah 4:10**

3. You give honor where honor is due.

No matter where you are in life right now, honor where you are on the way to where you're going. Pastor Steven Furtick says, "What's next in your life is always connected to what's now." Do everything with excellence and integrity. The more honor you show, the more honor you'll receive.

If you're working for someone, but your dream is to have your own company one day, then be the kind of employee you want to attract. Speak highly of your employer, arrive early, give your best performance, keep your office clean and tidy, do more than what's expected of you. Steven Furtick continued by saying, "What you're doing right now and how you're doing it is the most important thing about what God will give you next. When you honor what God is doing now, you'll be

237

prepared for what's next."

Above all else, honor God. Show Him how much you value Him, need Him and depend on Him by scheduling Him in your morning routine. Make Him the first priority of your day before anything and anyone can steal your time. Block time on your calendar and stick with your appointment as if you had a planned meeting with your most admirable mentor. You wouldn't dare think of just not showing up, canceling, or forgetting this highly anticipated date. Treat your Heavenly Father with that kind of respect and reverence.

Proverbs 3:9 tells us to, "Honor the Lord with your wealth…" (NIV). You can't give away something—with an honoring heart—without God giving you *more* in return. That's the way the Kingdom of God works.

Successful people are not generous because they're successful; they're successful because they're generous. Self-made billionaire, John Templeton said that successful people are often taught to be go-getters, but instead should be go-givers.

American philanthropist Andrew Carnegie set the bar for giving by saying, "No man can become rich without himself enriching others." Carnegie declared, "The man who dies rich dies disgraced."

Have you ever noticed that generous people seem to have more than enough? They distribute what they have, yet their lives are filled with more treasures, wealth, and riches. Anne Frank said, "No one has ever become poor from giving." That's because you cannot outgive God. He responds favorably to a generous heart. He will always bless you in return with more than what you've given. It's the law of sowing and reaping. The Bible says, "It's possible to give and yet become richer" (Proverbs 11:24, TLB).

The wonderful thing about generosity is that anyone can become a generous person no matter where they are in life. We have so much more to offer this world than just financial resources. We have time, attention, talents, aid, encouragement, experiences, prayer, and lessons learned. It's the significance, not the size, of your giving that matters.

"There is more happiness in giving than in receiving." - Acts 20:35b, GNT

Bottom line: Your contribution to the world is to be measured by something more than the size of your investment portfolio. Tap into a higher way of living by adopting this habit today. Instead of always praying for a miracle, become someone's miracle. When the bill arrives at lunch today, offer to pay for your co-worker's meal. When you can't fit another pair of shoes in your closet, give a beautiful pair to a single mom. When you mow your lawn, offer to mow the elderly widow's lawn as well. When you grab a cup of coffee on your way to work, buy the cup for the person standing in line behind you.

When God finds someone who is a consistent giver, get ready! When you invest your money into someone else's dream, you actually help yourself more than you help them. You strategically place yourself in a position to receive from God! What you make happen for others, God will make happen for you!

"A man's harvest in life depends entirely upon the seeds that he sows." - Galatians 6:7 Phillips Translation

And there you have it, take responsibility, form successful daily habits, and honor God. As a result, you'll be on the road to success.

It happened for me. With the five habits I practice every day before eight o'clock in the morning, I developed a dream routine that has led me to where I am today.

Today when people ask, "How do you know so many motivational phrases and quotes?" Every day I listen to a motivational message.

"How do you have the confidence to speak to thousands of people?" Every day in my prayer/meditation time I make my declarations of confidence and courage. "How do you have the energy to fly overseas, speak in conferences, and never have jet-lag?" Every day I incorporate exercise in my routine. Most people ask me the same question concerning my dreams and goals, "Why is it that everything you write down seems to happen?" Again, every day I review my list of dreams and goals. Whatever you keep before your eyes will eventually show up in your life.

The question I get more than anything, "How do you have *time* to do all these things every single day?" We make time for what's most important to us. The Pareto Principle, also known as the 80-20 Rule, suggests that 20% of your activities will produce 80% of your results. My personal daily five only takes up about 15-20% of my entire day. I'm finished by 8:00 in the morning. If you want to see change in your life, change something you do each day.

Remember, somebody in need is waiting on the other side of your obedience. Your new lifestyle of discipline and successful habits begins by conquering your covers, winning the battle of the bed, and practicing mind over mattress. The secret of your future is hidden in your daily routine. I'm cheering you on to get a routine that leads to your dreams.

ENDNOTES

1. Maxwell, John. Today Matters. Hatchett Book Group, 2004.
2. Tracy, Brian. The Power of Discipline. Simple Truths, 2008.
3. Stewart, James B. "Facebook has 50 minutes of your time each day. It wants more." The New York Times, May 5, 2016. https://www.nytimes.com/2016/05/06/business/facebook-bends-the-rules-of-audience-engagement-to-its-advantage.html. Accessed June 2018.
4. Reuters. "U.S. Commuters Spend About 42 Hours a Year Stuck in Traffic Jams." Newsweek, August 26, 2015. http://www.newsweek.com/us-commuters-spend-about-42-hours-year-stuck-traffic-jams-365970. Accessed June 2018.
5. "How You Will Spend Your Average Life Expectancy of 78 Years." Chegg Study. https://www.chegg.com/homework-help/questions-and-answers/spend-average-life-expectancy-78-years-19-according-american-bureau-labor-statistics-devot-q5869419. Accessed July 2018.
6. Tillman, Vicki. "3 Ways to Stop Wasting Your Life." Vicki Tillman Coaching, February 27, 2017. http://vickitillmancoaching.com/3-ways-to-stop-wasting-your-life/. Accessed June 2018.
7. Ware, Bronnie. "Regrets of the Dying." www.bronnieware.com/blog/regrets-of-the-dying/. Accessed July 2018.
8. Jobs, Steve. Steve Jobs: His Own Words and Wisdom. Cupertino Silicon Valley Press, 2011.
9. Cummings, Paul. "Stop Wasting Your Life." Paul Cummings. December 28, 2017, https://www.paulcummings.com/blog/stop-wasting-your-life. Accessed June 2018.
10. Shontell, Alyson. "80% Hate Their Jobs—But Should You Choose A Passion Or A Paycheck?" Business Insider. October 4, 2010, http://www.businessinsider.com/what-do-you-do-when-you-hate-your-job-2010-10. Accessed July 2018.
11. Koblin, John. "How Much Do We Love TV?" The New York Times. June 30, 2016, https://www.nytimes.com/2016/07/01/business/media/nielsen-survey-media-viewing.html. Accessed July 2018.
12. Sicinski, Adam. "Are You Living a Life of Endless Excuses? Here's How to Shop!" IQMatrix, https://blog.iqmatrix.com/a-life-of-excuses. Accessed July 2018.
13. "Jim Rohn Best Life Ever Full Length." YouTube, uploaded by Dale K. February 1, 2015. www.youtube.com/watch?v=l3AYRBTeGaQ.
14. Ibid.
15. "Reprogram Your Mind (A Must See Motivational Video)." YouTube, uploaded by Laws of Attraction Coaching, November 23, 2017, https://www.youtube.com/watch?v=tXP-JXo-1Dxs.

16. Elkins, Kathleen. "A man who spent 5 years studying millionaires found one of the most important wealth-building habits starts first thing in the morning." Business Insider. April 7, 2016, http://www.businessinsider.com/rich-people-wake-up-early-2016-4. Accessed July 2018.
17. Duhigg, Charles. The Power of Habit. Random House, 2012.
18. Neal, Benjamin. "8 Super-Successful People Who Meditate Daily." Pakwired. September 24, 2015, https://pakwired.com/8-super-successful-people-who-meditate-daily/. Accessed June 2018.
19. Ibid.
20. Barker, Alex. "The Surprising 'Superpower' Billionaires Want That You May Already Have." Entrepreneur. July 27, 2015, https://www.entrepreneur.com/article/247434. Accessed July 2018.
21. "Ashton Kutcher Speech at 2013 Teen Choice Awards." YouTube, uploaded by Wanda Thompson, August 15, 2013, www.youtube.com/watch?v=lkbroJKbK08.
22. "How To Build Your Vision From The Ground Up | Q&A With Bishop T.D. Jakes." YouTube, uploaded by Official Steven Furtick, October 26, 2017, www.youtube.com/watch?v=QVGk_jwyBXI.
23. Cuban, Mark. "Success and Motivation P4." Blog Maverick. May 25, 2004, www.blog-maverick.com/2011/04/07/shark-tank-success-motivation/. Accessed July 2018.
24. Hyatt, Michael. "5 Reasons Why You Should Commit Your Goals to Writing." Michael Hyatt. January 3, 2014, www.michaelhyatt.com/5-reasons-why-you-should-commit-your-goals-to-writing/. Accessed July 2018.
25. Jaslow, Ryan. "CDC: 80 percent of American adults don't get recommended exercise." CBS News. May 3, 2013, www.cbsnews.com/news/cdc-80-percent-of-american-adults-dont-get-recommended-exercise/. Accessed July 2018.
26. Duhigg, Charles. The Power of Habit. Random House, 2012.
27. Canfield, Jack. The Successful Principles. Collins Publishers, 2004.
28. Ibid.
29. Schwartz, David J. The Magic of Big Thinking. Touchstone, 1987.
30. Bristol, Claude M. The Magic of Believing. Pocket Books, 1991.
31. "Jim Rohn Best Life Ever Full Length." YouTube, uploaded by Dale K. February 1, 2015. www.youtube.com/watch?v=l3AYRBTeGaQ.
32. Ibid.
33. Canfield, Jack. The Success Principles. Collins Publishers, 2004.
34. Pierce, Stacia. "If You're Not Manifesting What You Want, You've Been Journaling Wrong." Stacia's Success Blog. www.lifecoach2women.com/main/if-youre-not-manifesting-what-you-want-youve-been-journaling-wrong/. Accessed July 2018.
35. Pierce, Stacia. "12 Reasons to Keep a Journal." Huffington Post. December 6, 2017, www.huffingtonpost.com/stacia-pierce/12-reasons-to-keep-a-jour_b_4774745.html. Accessed July 2018.
36. "Small Things, Big Difference: Week 1 - "Your One Word" with Craig Groeschel – LifeChurch.tv" YouTube, uploaded by Life.Church. January 6, 2014. www.youtube.com/watch?v=mXZYMAh-dG0.
37. Weissman, Jordan. "The Decline of the American Book Lover." The Atlantic. January

21, 2014, www.theatlantic.com/business/archive/2014/01/the-decline-of-the-american-book-lover/283222/. Accessed July 2018.

38. National Endowment of the Arts. The Office of Research & Analysis. (2007) ."To Read or Not To Read: A Question of National Consequence." Washington D.C.: www.arts.gov/sites/default/files/ToRead.pdf. Accessed July 2018.

39. Blakemore, Erin. "One in Four Americans Didn't Read a Book Last Year." Smithsonian. September 2, 2016. www.smithsonianmag.com/smart-news/one-four-americans-didnt-read-book-last-year-180960340/. Accessed July 2018.

40. News Desk. "75% of self-made millionaires report reading at least 2 books a month." Global Village Space. October 26, 2016. www.globalvillagespace.com/75-of-self-made-millionaires-report-reading-at-least-2-books-a-month/. Accessed July 2018.

41. Canfield, Jack. The Success Principles. Collins Publishers, 2004.

42. Merle, Andrew, "The Reading Habits of Ultra-Successful People." Huffington Post. April 14, 2016, www.huffingtonpost.com/andrew-merle/the-reading-habits-of-ul-t_b_9688130.html. Accessed July 2018.

43. "Jim Rohn Best Life Ever Full Length." YouTube, uploaded by Dale K. February 1, 2015. www.youtube.com/watch?v=l3AYRBTeGaQ.

44. Merle, Andrew. "The Reading Habits of Ultra-Successful People." Huffington Post. December 6, 2017, www.huffingtonpost.com/andrew-merle/the-reading-habits-of-ul-t_b_9688130.html. Accessed July 2018.

45. Move Forward Each Day by 1% | Th Power Of Slow Progress In Life." YouTube, uploaded by Absolute Motivation. December 20, 2016. www.youtube.com/watch?v=StTQzAE-3orI.

46. Corley, Tom. Rich Habits: The Daily Success Habits of Wealthy Individuals. Langdon Street Press, 2010.

47. "John Maxwell's Young Readers." YouTube, uploaded by JohnMaxwellCo. May 3, 2011, www.youtube.com/watch?v=Q2T4m78Q8pE&feature=youtu.be.

48. Tracy, Brian. Maximum Achievement: Strategies and Skills that Will Unlock Your Hidden Powers to Succeed. Simon Schuster, 1993.

49. Howes, Lewis. The School of Greatness. Rodale Books, 2015.

50. Bradberry, Travis. "14 Things Ridiculously Successful People Do Every Day." Inc. May 11, 2017. www.inc.com/travis-bradberry/14-things-ridiculously-successful-people-do-every-day.html. Accessed June 2018.

51. Ibid.

52. Allen, James. "Your Mental Attitude." James Allen Library. www.jamesallenlibrary.com/authors/james-allen/above-lifes-turmoil/your-mental-attitude. Accessed July 2018.

53. Mosley, J. Bruce. "A Controlled Trial of Arthroscopic Surgery for Osteoarthritis of the Knee." The New England Journal of Medicine. July 11, 2002. www.nejm.org/doi/full/10.1056/NEJMoa013259. Accessed July 2018.

54. Merle, Andrew, "The Reading Habits of Ultra-Successful People." Huffington Post. April 14, 2016, www.huffingtonpost.com/andrew-merle/the-reading-habits-of-ul-t_b_9688130.html. Accessed July 2018.

55. "Automobile University by Zig Ziglar." Get Motivation. www.getmotivation.com/motivationblog/2014/08/automobile-university-by-zig-ziglar/. Accessed July 2018

56. Dooley, Erin. "Here's How Much Time Americans Waste in Traffic." ABC News. August 26, 2015, www.abcnews.go.com/US/time-americans-waste-traffic/story?id=33313765. Accessed June 2018.

57. Steel, Mitch W. "Ten Great Life Lessons from a Legend; Coach John Wooden." Succcess. March 9, 2009. succcess.org/2009/03/09/ten-great-life-lessons-from-a-living-legend-coach-john-wooden/. Accessed July 2018.

58. Cardone, Grant. Be Obsessed or Be Average. Portfolio, 2016.

59. Amen, Daniel. Change Your Brain, Change Your Life. Harmony, 1998.

60. Jang, Meena. "iHeartRadio Awards 2015: Justin Timberlake Addresses Critics, Says 'Their Words Will Fade'." March 29, 2015, www.hollywoodreporter.com/news/justin-timberlake-receives-innovator-award-785158. Accessed July 2018.

61. Huffington, Arianna. Thrive: The Third Metric to Redefining Success and Creating a Life of Well-Being, Wisdom, and Wonder. Harmony. 2014.

62. Hoque, Faisal. "Why Extremely Successful People Swear by this 5 minute Daily Habit." Business Insider. November 19, 2015, www.businessinsider.com/why-extremely-successful-people-swear-by-this-5-minute-daily-habit-2015-11. Accessed June 2018.

63. "The Importance of Gratitude." UMASS Dartmoth. www.umassd.edu/counseling/for-parents/recommendedreadings/theimportanceofgratitude/. Accessed July 2018.

64. DeJoria, John Paul. "This billionaire follows the same routine every morning, no matter where he is in the world." Business Insider. March 31, 2015, www.businessinsider.com/john-paul-dejorias-morning-routine-2015-3. Accessed July 2018.

65. Rich, Kimberly. "The Antidote to Regret." YouTube, uploaded by TEDx Talks. November 13, 2017. www.youtube.com/watch?v=MZV10lsvurM.

66. John Goddard: The World's Greatest Goal Achiever. johngoddard.info/. Accessed July 2018.

67. "Reprogram Your Mind (A Must See Motivational Video)." YouTube, uploaded by Laws of Attraction Coaching, November 23, 2017, https://www.youtube.com/watch?v=tXP-JXo-1Dxs.

68. Canfield, Jack. The Success Principles. Collins Publishers, 2004.

69. Tilawan. How to Keep Fit, Be Healthy & Stay Young: The Secrets to Living a Healthy and Youthful Life. AuthorHouse. 2016.

70. Canfield, Jack; Hansen, Mark Victor. The Aladdin Factor. Berkley Book. 1995.

71. Maxwell, John. Put Your Dreams to the Test. Thomas Nelson, 2011.

72. "MJ's 'Manifesto,' Penned in 1979." CBS News, September 08, 2013. www.cbsnews.com/news/mjs-manifesto-penned-in-1979/. Accessed July 2018.

73. Morrisey, Mary. "The Power of Writing Down Your Goals and Dreams." Huffington Post. September 14, 2016, www.huffingtonpost.com/marymorrissey/the-power-of-writing-down_b_12002348.html. Accessed June 2018.

74. Power, Rhett. "3 Things Ultra-Productive People Do Differently." Inc. July 16, 2015, www.inc.com/rhett-power/3-things-ultra-productive-people-do-differently.html. Accessed June 2018.

75. Tracy, Brian. "Successful People Are Self Disciplined." Brian Tracy International. www.briantracy.com/blog/time-management/successful-people-are-self-discipline-high-value-personal-management/. Accessed July 2018.

76. Cardone, Grant. The 10X Factor. Wiley, 2011.

77. Miller, Lindsey. "Dad wouldn't pay his son to do chores; what he did instead made his son a millionaire." Famifi. July 11, 2017. www.famifi.com/28180/dad-wouldn-t-pay-his-son-do-do-chores-what-he-did-instead-made-his-son-a-millionaire. Accessed July 2018.

78. "Steve Harvey–Vision Boards" YouTube, uploaded by Yolande Marie. September 23, 2014. www.youtube.com/watch?v=pJNed-owcP8.

79. "Emma Stone Biography." Biography. December 11, 2017. www.biography.com/people/emma-stone-20874773. Accessed July 2018.

80. Weiner, Jonah. "Drake: High Times at the YOLO Estate." Rolling Stone. February 13, 2014, www.rollingstone.com/music/music-news/drake-high-times-at-the-yolo-estate-72518/. Accessed July 2018.

81. Canfield, Jack. The Success Principles. Collins Publishers, 2004.

82. Fabrikant, Geraldine. "Talking Money With: Sarah Jessica Parker; From a Start On Welfare To Riches In the City." The New York Times. July 30, 2000. www.nytimes.com/2000/07/30/business/talking-money-with-sarah-jessica-parker-start-welfare-riches-city.html. Accessed July 2018.

83. Maxwell, John. The 21 Irrefutable Laws of Leadership: Follow Them and People Will Follow You. Thomas Nelson, 1998.

84. "The Dillard Commencement." YouTube, uploaded by Durell Jacque. May 9, 2015. www.youtube.com/watch?v=_WG3nDda6D8.

85. Gillett, Rachel. "How 19 highly successful people stay in shape." Business Insider. April 18, 2016. www.businessinsider.com/exercise-routines-of-highly-successful-people-2016-4. Accessed July 2018.

86. "Diet and weight loss statistics." Fitness for Weight Loss, www.fitnessforweightloss.com/diet-and-weight-loss-statistics/. Accessed July 2018.

87. Ibid.

88. Ibid.

89. "Stress and Anxiety Interfere With Sleep." Anxiety and Depression Association of America. adaa.org/understanding-anxiety/related-illnesses/other-related-conditions/stress/stress-and-anxiety-interfere. Accessed July 2018.

90. Ferris, Timothy. The 4-Hour Body. Harmony, 2010.

91. D'Onfro, Jillian, "Arnold Schwarzenegger asked Mark Zuckerberg about his workout routine—Here's what Zuck said." Business Insider. June 30, 2015, www.businessinsider.com/mark-zuckerberg-workout-routine-2015-6. Accessed July 2018.

92. Duvauchelle, Joshua. "5 Consequences of Not Exercising." Livestrong, September 11, 2017. www.livestrong.com/article/501683-5-consequences-of-not-exercising/. Accessed June 2018.

93. O'Meara, Alex. "The Percent of People Who Regain Weight After Rapid Weight Loss and the Risks of Doing So." Livestrong. July 18, 2017, www.livestrong.com/article/438395-the-percentage-of-people-who-regain-weight-after-rapid-weight-loss-risks/. Accessed July 2018.

94. Johnson, Chalene. "11 Tips for a Successfully Fit Life." Spry Living. June 13, 2012, spryliving.com/articles/11-tips-for-a-successfully-fit-life/. Accessed June 2018.

95. Cotton, Adrien. "How Language Impacts Your Health + Fitness: Channeling Your Self-

Talk and Inner Voice." Alexandria Stylebook. November 18, 2016. alexandriastylebook.com/language-impacts-health-fitness-channeling-self-talk-inner-voice/. Accessed July 2018.

96. Foroux, Darius. "10 Habits of Unsuccessful People You Don't Want to Copy." Darius Foroux. January 21, 2016, dariusforoux.com/10-habits-of-unsuccessful-people-you-dont-want-to-copy/. Accessed June 2018.

97. Horsager, David. The Daily Edge: Simple Strategies to Increase Efficiency and Make an Impact Every Day. Berrett-Koehler Publishing, 2015.

98. Luszczyk, Heather. "The toxic effects of complaining." Natural Healing News. February 28, 2012, naturalhealingnews.com/the-toxic-effects-of-complaining/#.W0AUaNJKhPY. Accessed June 2018.

99. Grossman, Samantha. "The 14 Worst Kinds of Late People." Time. August 7, 2015, time.com/3984571/worst-types-of-late-people/. Accessed June 2018/

100. West, John. "Being late says a lot about you, and none of it's good." InfoWorld. March 15, 2007, www.infoworld.com/article/2643289/it-careers/being-late-says-a-lot-about-you—and-none-of-it-s-good.html. Accessed June 2018/

101. Ziglar, Zig. See You At The Top. Pelican Publishing Company, 1974.

102. Corley, Thomas. "I Spent 5 Years Studying Poor People and Here Are 4 Destructive Money Habits They Had." Rich Habits. September 22, 2015, richhabits.net/i-spent-5-years-studying-poor-people-and-here-are-4-destructive-money-habits-they-had/. Accessed June 2018.

103. Corley, Thomas. "My 5-year study of rich and poor people found 4 types of habits that will keep you from getting rich." Business Insider. October 2, 2015, www.businessinsider.com/types-of-habits-that-will-keep-you-from-getting-rich-2015-10. Accessed June 2018.

104. Radwan, M. Farouk. "What causes fears and phobias?" Know Myself, www.2knowmyself.com/What_causes_fears_and_phobias. Accessed July 2018.

105. Lake, Rebecca. "Television Statistics: 23 Mind-Numbing Facts to Watch." Credit Donkey. November 16, 2015, www.creditdonkey.com/television-statistics.html. Accessed June 2018.

106. Rowles, Dustin. "TV Kills: Sobering Statistics On The TV Watching Habits Of the Average American." UpRoxx. January 29, 2015, uproxx.com/tv/tv-kills-sobering-statistics-on-the-tv-watching-habits-of-the-average-american/. Accessed June 2018.

107. Corley, Thomas. "I Spent 5 Years Studying Poor People and Here Are 4 Destructive Money Habits They Had." Rich Habits. September 22, 2015. http://richhabits.net/i-spent-5-years-studying-poor-people-and-here-are-4-destructive-money-habits-they-had/. Accessed June 2018.

108. "Overweight & Obesity Statistics." National Institute of Diabetes and Digestive and Kidney Diseases. August 2017, www.niddk.nih.gov/health-information/health-statistics/overweight-obesity. Accessed June 2018.

109. Jaines, Kira. "Ten Reasons People Do Not Exercise." Livestrong. July 18, 2017, www.livestrong.com/article/370670-ten-reasons-people-do-not-exercise/. Accessed June 2018.

110. Psychologies. "Why we love to gossip." Psychologies. December 7, 2011, www.psychologies.co.uk/self/why-we-love-to-gossip.html. Accessed July 2018.

111. Murphy, Jr., Bill. "10 Things Unsuccessful People Never Stop Doing." Inc. September 1, 2015, www.inc.com/bill-murphy-jr/10-things-really-unhappy-and-unsuccessful-people-never-stop-doing.html. Accessed July 2018.

112. Pavlina, Steve. "Do It Now." Steve Pavlina. November 28, 2005, www.stevepavlina.com/blog/2005/11/do-it-now/. Accessed July 2018.

113. Estroff Marano, Hara." Procrastination: Ten Things To Know." Psychology Today. August 23, 2003, www.psychologytoday.com/us/articles/200308/procrastination-ten-things-know. Accessed July 2018.

114. Swanson, Ana. "The real reasons you procrastinate—and how to stop." The Washington Post. April 27, 2016, https://www.washingtonpost.com/news/wonk/wp/2016/04/27/why-you-cant-help-read-this-article-about-procrastination-instead-of-doing-your-job/?noredirect=on&utm_term=.019c9c333e90. Accessed June 2018.

115. Luciani, Joseph. "Why 80 Percent of New Year's Resolutions Fail." U.S. News and World Report. December 29. 2015, health.usnews.com/health-news/blogs/eat-run/articles/2015-12-29/why-80-percent-of-new-years-resolutions-fail. Accessed June 2018.

116. Diamond, Dan. "Just 8% of People Achieve Their New Year's Resolutions." Fox25News. January 1, 2014, okcfox.com/archive/just-8-of-people-achieve-their-new-years-resolutions-heres-how-they-do-it. Accessed June 2018.

117. Munroe, Myles. Maximizing Your Potential. Destiny Image, 1992.

118. Baer, Drake. "How 9 Incredibly Successful People Define Success." Business Insider. June 2, 2014, www.businessinsider.com/how-9-incredibly-successful-people-define-success-2014-5. Accessed July 2018.

119. Ziglar, Zig. Born to Win! Find Your Success Code. Made For Success Publishing, 2017.

120. Covey, Stephen. The 7 Habits of Highly Effective People. Free Press, 2004.

121. Nightingale, Earl. "The Strangest Secret Article." Nightingale Conant. www.nightingale.com/articles/the-strangest-secret/. Accessed July 2018.

122. "More Quotes by Charles Kendall Adams." Forbes Quotes. 2015, www.forbes.com/quotes/author/charles-kendall-adams/. Accessed July 2018.

123. "Where is Haverhill, Massachusetts? Including History, Facts and Figure." Haverall. USA. www.haverhillusa.com/whereishaverhill.html. Accessed July 2018.

124. Saludo, Ricardo. "How Akio Morita's Rice Flameout Led to Sony." Inc. November 12, 2015. inc-asean.com/technology/how-akio-moritas-rice-flameout-led-to-sony/. Accessed July 2018.

125. Trapani, Gina. "Jerry Seinfeld's Productivity Secret." Lifehacker. July 24, 2007, lifehacker.com/281626/jerry-seinfelds-productivity-secret. Accessed July 2018.

126. Clear, James. "The Difference Between Professionals and Amateurs." James Clear, jamesclear.com/professionals-and-amateurs. Accessed July 2018.

127. Macomber, Debbie. "A Day in the Life of Debbie Macomber." Female First. August 11, 2017. www.femalefirst.co.uk/books/debbie-macomber-any-dream-will-do-1081374.html. Accessed July 2018.

128. Burghate, Sonal. "Jan Koum and Brian Acton: Founders of WhatsApp." Insights Success. www.insightssuccess.com/jan-koum-and-brian-acton-founders-of-whatsapp/. Accessed July 2018.

129. "Milton Hershey Biography." Biography. A&E Television Networks. April 27, 2017,

www.biography.com/people/milton-hershey-9337133. Accessed July 2018.

130. Osteen, Joel. Break Out! 5 Keys to Go Beyond Your Barriers and Live an Extraordinary Life. FaithWords, 2013.

131. "Ziglar on Ethics: Adapted From A Conversation on Character." Ziglar, 2007. www.super-super.com/hpe405/page1/files/Ethics.pdf. Accessed July 2018.

132. Maxwell, John. Today Matters. Center Street, 2005.

133. 133 Lier, Dan. "How to Create Consistency in Your Life." YouTube, uploaded by Dan Lier. August 10, 2015. www.youtube.com/watch?v=Uvnus5HIInk.

134. Maxwell, John. "Take 5." The John Maxwell Company. August 18, 2014, www.john-maxwell.com/blog/take-5. Accessed June 2018.

135. Hardy, Darren. The Compound Effect. SUCCESS Books, 2010.

136. 1 Kings 18:41-45, Author's paraphrase.

137. Bracke, Marissa. "The Three Day Rule of Effective Habits." Melissa Bracke. April 18, 2011, marissabracke.com/three-day-rule-effective-habits. Accessed July 2018.

138. Martin, Lauren. "Scientists Say It Only Takes 66 Days to Change Your Life, If You're Strong Enough." Elite Daily. October 6, 2014, www.elitedaily.com/life/motivation/need-stop-bad-habit-need-66-days/784244. Accessed July 2018.

139. Yates, Brad. "WATCH: 'The Will to Do It.'" Huffington Post. August 30, 2013, www.huffingtonpost.com/brad-yates/eft-tapping_b_3839655.html. Accessed July 2018.

140. Canfield, Jack. The Success Principles. Collins Publishers, 2004.

141. Maxwell, John. The 15 Invaluable Laws of Growth. Center Street, 2012.

142. Hardy, Darren. The Compound Effect. SUCCESS Books, 2010.

ABOUT TERRI

For years, Terri Savelle Foy's life was average. She had no dreams to pursue. Each passing day was just a repeat of the day before. Finally, with a marriage in trouble and her life falling apart, Terri made a change. She began to pursue God like never before, develop a new routine and discovered the power of having a dream and purpose.

As Terri started to recognize her own dreams and goals, she simply wrote them down and reviewed them consistently. This written vision became a road map to drive her life. As a result, those dreams are now a reality.

Terri has become the Founder of an international Christian ministry. She is the host of the Live Your Dreams television broadcast, an author, a conference speaker, and a success coach to hundreds of thousands of people all over the world. Her best-selling books Make Your Dreams Bigger than Your Memories, Imagine Big, and Pep Talk have helped people discover how to overcome the hurts of the past and see the possibilities of a limitless future. Her weekly podcast is a lifeline of hope and inspiration to people around the world.

Terri Savelle Foy is a cheerleader of dreams and is convinced that "if you can dream it, God can do it." She is known across the globe as a world-class motivator of hope and success through her transparent and humorous teaching style. Terri's unique ability to communicate success strategies in a simple and practical way has awakened the dreams of the young and old alike.

Terri shares from personal experience the biblical concepts of using the gift of the imagination to reach full potential in Jesus Christ. From stay-at-home moms to business executives, Terri consistently inspires others to go after their dreams. With step-by-step instruction and the inspiration to follow through, people are fueled with the passion to complete their life assignment down to the last detail (see John 17:4).

Terri and her husband, Rodney Foy, have been married since 1991, and are the parents of a beautiful redheaded daughter, Kassidi Cherie. They live near Dallas, Texas.

MORE BY THE AUTHOR

Declutter Your Way to Success

Dream it. Pin it. Live it.

Imagine Big

*Make Your Dreams Bigger
Than Your Memories*

Pep Talk

The Leader's Checklist

Untangled

You're Valuable to God

TERRI.COM

WHAT YOU CAN FIND ON
THE WEBSITE:

- Partnership growth tracks
- Weekly podcast teaching
- Resource specials
- 24/7 access to online video teaching
- Encouraging blog posts
- Enroll to get your weekly "pep talk" straight to your inbox

www.terri.com

VISION101.ONLINE

Vision 101 is not for everyone. This is a one year coaching program put together by Terri for the person who desires discipline in their life. After completing this "mentorship" program, your life will not be where it is today, next year at this time.

In *Vision 101* you'll get, a step-by-step guide to discover your passion and purpose and the keys to be more productive, stress-free, and healthy. You'll also receive a personal success growth plan, proven methods to organize your life and tools to grow spiritually, mentally,

---

VISION 101 IS A 12-MODULE ONLINE COURSE THAT SHOWS YOU HOW TO:

- Achieve the dreams and goals in your heart
- Conquer debilitating procrastination
- Develop discipline in key areas
- Make each day productive
- Be effective instead of busy
- Obtain vital habits to succeed in life

ENROLL FOR *VISION 101* **AT** <u>VISION101.ONLINE</u>

PEP TALK

GIVING YOURSELF A PEP TALK CONSISTENTLY AND INTENTIONALLY IS KEY TO ACHIEVING YOUR DREAMS.

Why? Because your words are powerful and the words you speak about yourself are even more powerful. Discover what to say from God's Word about your freedom, faith, finances, family, fitness, and your future dreams and goals in my book *Pep Talk*.

WHEN THE VISION IS CLEAR, THE RESULTS WILL APPEAR.

DREAM IT. PIN IT. LIVE IT.

MAKE VISION BOARDS WORK FOR YOU!

Clarity about your dreams is the single most important step to success! Discover how vision boards work, what to do after you've made them, and the hidden key to living your dreams.

STAY CONNECTED

@terrisavellefoy

 youtube.com/terrisavellefoy

 pinterest.com/terrisavellefoy

 facebook.com/terrisavellefoy

 twitter.com/terrisavellefoy

 instagram.com/terrisavellefoy

MAILING ADDRESS:

Terri Savelle Foy Ministries
P.O.Box 1959
Rockwall, Texas 75087

CALL NOW:

1-877-661-TSFM (8736)